Pocket Verses

Pocket Verses

Learning, Loving and Living the Word of God

Sherry Stokes

XULON PRESS

Xulon Press
2301 Lucien Way #415
Maitland, FL 32751
407.339.4217
www.xulonpress.com

© 2021 by Sherry Stokes

All rights reserved solely by the author. The author guarantees all contents are original and do not infringe upon the legal rights of any other person or work. No part of this book may be reproduced in any form without the permission of the author. The views expressed in this book are not necessarily those of the publisher.

Due to the changing nature of the Internet, if there are any web addresses, links, or URLs included in this manuscript, these may have been altered and may no longer be accessible. The views and opinions shared in this book belong solely to the author and do not necessarily reflect those of the publisher. The publisher therefore disclaims responsibility for the views or opinions expressed within the work.

Unless otherwise indicated, Scripture quotations taken from the Holy Bible, New International Version (NIV). Copyright © 1973, 1978, 1984, 2011 by Biblica, Inc.™. Used by permission. All rights reserved.

Scripture quotations taken from the New American Standard Bible (NASB). Copyright © 1960, 1962, 1963, 1968, 1971, 1972, 1973, 1975, 1977, 1995 by The Lockman Foundation. Used by permission. All rights reserved.

Scripture quotations taken from the English Standard Version (ESV). Copyright © 2001 by Crossway, a publishing ministry of Good News Publishers. Used by permission. All rights reserved.

Scripture quotations taken from the Complete Jewish Bible (CJB). Copyright © 1998 by David H. Stern. All rights reserved. No portion of this book may be reproduced, stored in a retrieval system, or transmitted in any form or by any means without prior written permission of the publisher.

Scripture quotations taken from the Contemporary English Version (CEV). Copyright © 1995 American Bible Society. Used by permission. All rights reserved.

Scripture quotations taken from the Amplified Bible (AMP). Copyright © 1954, 1958, 1962, 1964, 1965, 1987 by The Lockman Foundation. Used by permission. All rights reserved.

Scripture quotations taken from the Holy Bible, New Living Translation (NLT). Copyright ©1996, 2004, 2007 by Tyndale House Foundation. Used by permission of Tyndale House Publishers, Inc.

Scripture quotations taken from the King James Version (KJV) – *public domain*.

Scripture quotations taken from The Message (MSG). Copyright © 1993, 1994, 1995, 1996, 2000, 2001, 2002. Used by permission of NavPress Publishing Group. Used by permission. All rights reserved.

The New Testament in Modern English by J.B Phillips copyright © 1960, 1972 J. B. Phillips. Administered by The Archbishops' Council of the Church of England. Used by Permission.

Paperback ISBN-13: 978-1-6628-2105-9
Ebook ISBN-13: 978-1-6628-2106-6

To my "babies", Trey, Cory, Andrew and Katy.
You have taught me so much
and brought me inexpressible joy.
I so deeply treasure each one of you;
I am blessed to be called your mom.
I love you guys, and I thank God for you.

To my husband, Todd,
who one day, out of the blue,
said to me, "Maybe it's time to come home".
With those words, I quit my job, stayed home,
and this new journey began.
Thank you for the opportunity to serve the
Lord this way.
I love you and I respect you.
You are my guy, and we will always be we.

To my Angie.
When I shared my verses with you,
when I told you my kids call them "pocket verses",
you confidently told me,
"That will be the name of your first book!"
All these years later, it is so.
You are a faithful, loving friend,
who let me know it's okay to be real.
You laugh with me. You cry with me.
I love you.

To my Jennifer.
I'll never forget the day you walked in
to the fourth-grade classroom.
Thank you for journeying authentically
through this life with me.
As iron sharpens iron.
I love you.

To all my ladies.
You who come each week to study God's Word with me.
I smile when I think of you.
To those who came and passed through quickly,
and those who have come and stayed awhile,
I love you all, and I'm so grateful for each one of you.

And to my mom,
who gave me my first Bible,
who faithfully lived out the words inside.
I love you, mama.

"When your words came,
I ate them;
They were my joy and my heart's delight,
For I bear Your name,
O LORD God Almighty."

~ Jeremiah 15:16 ~

Table of Contents

1. Introduction..................xiii
2. I Can Do It!....................1
3. The Pretty Room................5
4. New Clothes...................10
5. Healed and Helping............13
6. What's in Your Hand?..........15
7. Extraordinary Courage.........18
8. Calling Him Father............24
9. The Eternal Advocate..........26
10. Waking Up Hungry.............28
11. Then.........................33
12. One Thing I Know.............36
13. Leading the Way..............40
14. The Difference...............43
15. Delightful Counselors........47
16. A Light in the Dark..........49
17. Because They Trust...........52
18. Into His Ears................55
19. Morning Words................57
20. Fear and Faith...............61
21. Bad News.....................64
22. Rivers, Fires and Flames.....67
23. My Mighty Warrior............70
24. The Work of a Weaver.........72
25. Broken Yokes.................75

26. The Airport. 78
27. What Do I Do? 82
28. But As For Me 85
29. Don't Give Up 88
30. The Soldiers Clothes 91
31. Idols. 94
32. Fire in My Bones 97
33. Grace in the Wait 100
34. He Will Provide 103
35. The Promise Goes On 107
36. Torn Hearts 110
37. Seeing. 113
38. Believe. 116
39. He's Been So Good 119
40. First the Songs 121
41. Powerless 125
42. Where, When and Why 128
43. Old Clothes 133
44. Why We Remember 136
45. The Centurion Heard 140
46. He Has a Home 142
47. The Servants Knew 146
48. What Shall I Do With Jesus? 151
49. Come! 154
50. One Last Thing… 158
51. Conclusion 162

Introduction

I thought it was just another work day, like so many days before. But something happened this particular morning as I prepared to head out the door that I realize, as I look back now, changed the course of my life. Sounds rather dramatic, I know, but the change that began that morning is just about as dramatic as it gets.

I had been following Jesus for just a little over a year when I got a job at a Christian pre-school. I enjoyed my work very much and was thankful for it. I loved teaching the children about Jesus, and I had a wonderful boss who became a much-needed mentor for me.

During the months that I worked in this preschool, I was being drawn more and more to read God's Word. As I said, I was quite young in my faith, only about a year old, so this was a rather new idea, but it was one that I was very much desiring. In fact, I found myself hungering for time alone to read my Bible. This was clearly a work of the Holy Spirit!

However, with four young children to get up and ready for school, that time, particularly in the morning, was definitely not as much as I wanted. But I would get up early and read what I could, then get on with taking care of my kids and getting myself ready for work.

And so came that dramatic morning. Just before I walked out the door, I looked around my home, making sure everything was turned off and locked and in its place. As I scanned the kitchen and dining room area, my eyes fell upon my Bible which lay open on the table. A feeling washed over me that could only be described as sadness. Simply yet intensely I realized, I didn't want to go to work. I wanted to stay home and read and study. But that was not possible, not yet, so with one last glance, I turned, walked out my front door and went to work with that strange sadness in my heart.

Very early the next morning as I sat reading, a thought came to me. It was without a doubt a God-given thought. When I came across a verse that stuck out to me more than any others, I decided to write it down on a scrap piece of paper. Since I hadn't yet hidden God's Word in my heart, and I sure couldn't tote my big old study Bible around with me, (and, no, there were no Bible aps yet!), I put this wee treasure into my pocket and took it to work with me.

This soon became almost a daily habit. Any time a certain verse would grab my attention, whether it was comforting or confusing, convicting or simply amazing, I would write it down and put it in my pocket. Throughout the day I would pull it out and read it, pondering the words, thinking about them, memorizing them, contemplating what they meant for me. Slowly, I even began sharing them with people at work or folks I would meet in stores and such. Anytime, anywhere, I had a little snippet of God's Word with me.

That one morning so, so long ago, truly did change the course of my life. It was indeed a turning point. It was just a quiet, simple moment in time known to no one but

Introduction

me and the Lord, but the desire that He put it my heart in that moment was very real. These wee treasures soon made their way into my heart, my life, my journals – and now – into the pages of this book, these treasures that my kids began calling "pocket verses".

I am so honored and delighted to share some of these pocket verses with you, what they mean and and what they mean to me. These precious words come from the very heart of God. There are no words more valuable, more transformative, more worthy of discussion. God used them to teach me Who He is, who I am, and how to walk with Him in this world. He taught me how to love and to grow and to serve. The verses I pondered renewed my mind, my attitude and my spirit. And sometimes, yes, sometimes, they helped me to simply survive.

My Bible is the most precious earthly possession I own. The only thing more delightful than feasting on it for myself, is to share it with you. I do hope and pray that these verses will do for you what they did for me.

With love and for God's glory,
Sherry

I Can Do It!

> *"'Come to me, all you who are weary and burdened, and I will give you rest. Take my yoke upon you and learn from me, for I am gentle and humble in heart, and you will find rest for your souls.*
> *For my yoke is easy and my burden is light.'"*
> *~ Matthew 11:28-30, NIV ~*

In the spring of 2003, my daughter was just a few months away from her third birthday. During that time, I had, for quite awhile, been running from the Lord, so scared of Who He is and what might happen if I did respond to His obvious pursuing.

One day Katy was headed upstairs with her arms full of baby dolls. I walked along with her with my arms opened, positioned to catch her and the dolls, if need be, and told her several times, *"Let me help you, baby girl! Let mama carry the dolls for you!"* But, in her toddler independence, she adamantly replied, *"No, mommy, I do it myself!"*

I continued to walk beside her, up three steps, then four, all the while watching those dolls fall. While she was picking up one, another would fall from her wee arms. The whole time she kept insisting, *"I do it all by myself, mommy!"*

Finally, just about half way up, Katy suddenly turned and dumped all those dolls into my arms. As she began walking the rest of the way up the staircase, she said the most shocking thing. Shocking to my own stubborn heart, that is. I was stunned when I heard her shout out, *"Whew, now I can make it!"*

Now, I'm not sure what or how God did what He did in my mind and my heart in that moment, but I literally could not move. I stood there in the middle of that staircase watching my girl walk the rest of the way with ease, unburdened and carefree, and all I could do was to stand there holding those dolls. Somehow God took that scene and those words and He used them to show me Who He is and what He wanted so much to do for me. My own arms were so, so loaded down with such a heavy burden. Several heavy burdens, actually. And I was doing exactly what my Katy did with her dolls that day. I was rejecting the only Help that was truly available. I was ignoring the call to unburden myself, and to accept the rest that Jesus alone can offer. I was, in effect, saying to Jesus, *I can do it by myself!*

But that day on the stairs as I stood watching this scene unfold, considering all that the Holy Spirit was showing me in that moment, I found myself whispering, *"Could it really be that simple? Is it that easy?"* My thoughts were broken then, by the calling of my girl to bring the dolls and come and play!

Do we have any idea how good our Father is? How could He use such a simple thing to show me what I needed to do? How deep is His love for us? How gracious of Him to open my eyes and my heart and enable me to learn from Him that day. It will always be one of the most important and pivotal moments in my life because it began to change the way I viewed God. And years later, when I read this verse in Matthew, I remembered that day on the staircase with my Katy.

"Come unto me", Jesus says. This is the greatest invitation ever given. In man's desperate search for spiritual rest, for salvation of the soul, Jesus calls out, *Let me help you!* Stop striving. Quit attempting to save yourself. Trying to be good enough, to work hard enough, is exhausting. There is no greater burden than that of self-righteousness. Rejecting Christ's offer and continuing on in our own way will not bring rest! I know. I was so weighed down under my burden of sin.

Eventually I did come to Jesus. I stopped running from the conviction I felt. I did stop ignoring my need for a Saviour. I stopped trying to be 'good enough' on my own and to carry my burdens all by myself. I came to Him and called on Him with a repentant and contrite heart. I turned my life over to Him and I did indeed find rest for my soul. The kind of rest that only Jesus can give.

As time went on, God taught me something more from this staircase scene –

All too often, after we are saved, we revert back to that toddler stage. Over and over again I find myself bogged down with my arms full of life's burdens, telling God, *I can do it! I can carry these! I don't need Your help!* Now, to be honest, I may not actually say those words, and nor might you, but our actions speak clearly. We are trying to do everything ourselves, just like my daughter did that day. But I know that Jesus continues to walk patiently beside me, His arms open and ready to catch me, waiting for me to cast my burdens on Him. He continues to be here, whispering to my heart, *Let Me carry those for you, child.*

I am amazed at His patient persistence. He will not yank the load out of our arms, but, just like I did with my girl that day - to let her struggle till she made the choice - so the Father does with me. With all of us. Yes, He stays with us, urging us to come to Him. He is here right now, ready, willing and able to carry every burden. To carry you! And when we dump it all into His mighty arms, when we surrender it to Him, we can walk just as freely and unburdened as my Katy did that day. And we can say with her, *Whew, now I can make it!* I believe Peter puts it this way –

> **"Casting the whole of your care [all your anxieties, all your worries, all your concerns, once and for all] on Him, for He cares for you affectionately and cares about you watchfully."**
> **~ 1 Peter 5:7, Amplified Bible, Classic Edition (AMPC) ~**

The Pretty Room

*"As Jesus and His disciples were on their way,
He came to a village where a woman named Martha
opened her home to Him."*
~ Luke 10:38, NIV ~

As I began reading this familiar passage of scripture, the account of Jesus visiting Mary and Martha, I was amazed by the words of this verse and had to rest here awhile. What struck me was the phrase, **opened her home to Him.** Other translations, including the New American Standard Bible, use the phrase, **welcomed Him into her home**.

Now, I've learned many lessons on Mary sitting and Martha serving, which is the context of this verse, but this day it occurred to me that we can neither sit nor serve until we welcome Jesus in!

For those who have never opened their hearts to Christ, receiving Him as Lord and Saviour is the first step. Paul tells us in Romans 10:9-10, NIV –

*"That if you confess with your mouth, 'Jesus is Lord',
and believe in your heart that God raised Him from the
dead, you will be saved."*

If you have not done that, then I am praying for you. I pray that the Lord would open your heart to respond to His message of salvation by grace through faith. I pray the Holy Spirit would draw to Himself and bring you to that place of repentance and belief. If you sense that happening, then please call out to Jesus today!

But I prayed, then, *"What about for those of us who have made that decision? What does this mean for me and for all believers? What lesson can we learn from these precious words?"*

The answer didn't come right away. Off and on throughout the day while I went about my work, I would pull this verse out, read it again, and pray. I knew there was an application that I did not want to miss.

Later that afternoon I found myself remembering the years I cleaned houses for people. I was kind of laughing to myself as I recalled how almost every home had what I called "the pretty room". You know, the room that is almost never used. The fancy living room. Although why it is called a living room I'm not sure, because the only time it is ever used is when a special guest comes by!

Suddenly this picture of "the pretty room" connected with my pocket verse and I said out loud, *"God, that's what we do!"* Yes, we are born-again believers, Christ is indeed dwelling in us. (2 Cor 13:5, Gal 2:20). We have welcomed Him in, but that's as far as it goes. Oh, please don't get me wrong. Before I go on, I have to say that I believe based on the Word of God, that we get *all* of Jesus, all of His Spirit when we are saved. His work is complete and perfect! But all too often, we try to keep Jesus out of much of our lives. He is like the special guest in the pretty room. We open the door of our heart to Jesus, but we never welcome Him in to the kitchens and bedrooms and family rooms of our lives. We try to keep Him out of the places where decisions are made, schedules are organized, relationships are built and broken, money is spent, and real life happens.

It occurred to me that the time we sit with Jesus and the time we spend serving Him will be much more effective the more we welcome Him in. It's called submitting to Him. Surrendering our whole selves. We must open every part of our lives to Jesus. All the rooms, all the closets and tiny spaces.

Oh, we've got many excuses for why we don't. I know I do. I know I'm still working on some of them. I used to hope that God wouldn't open up that one cabinet, the real high one that no one ever uses, and definitely no one ever looks in! *No, God, don't peek in there! You see, there's sin hiding in there that I am not ready to acknowledge. Well, I don't call it sin. You'll find it stored in a couple of boxes marked 'an old habit' and 'just the way I am'. No, no, not that closet! There are masks in there that I still want to keep! You'll find them hanging in garment bags labelled 'hypocrisy' and 'hiding'. And that drawer filled with 'I want my own way' – please don't look in there, Jesus.*

The truth is, of course, He already knows it's in there. He sees all. He knows all. He is aware of every thought before we think it. He knows our words, our attitudes, our motives, our secret, sinful struggles and weaknesses. Nothing is hidden from Him. But in spite of it all, oh how He loves us! He loves us too much to leave those things in us; He wants to clean them out of us! It's the process of our ongoing sanctification!

So Martha opened her home to Jesus, and then she began complaining. She *was distracted by all the preparations that needed to be made.* (Luke 10:40a), and she grumbled right to Jesus' face! *"Lord, don't You care that my sister has left me to do all the work by myself? Tell her to help me!* (Luke 10:40b).

Yeah, that sounds awful, but I've been thinking about this, and it seems to me that Martha gets kind of a bad rap. Yes, I realize that she had a terrible attitude. She was caught up in her work instead of Who she was working for. She was wading around in self-pity that day. But what I admire about Martha, is that she welcomed Jesus not only into her home, but yes, even into her bad attitude! She didn't try to disguise it or lie about it. She didn't go all passive aggressive. She was honest with Jesus, completely honest. She let Him in to see who she really was and only then could she be taught the most valuable lesson. *"Martha, Martha", the Lord answered, "you are worried and upset about many things, but only one thing is needed. Mary has chosen what is better, and it will not be taken away from her."* (Luke 10:41-42)

The one thing that is needed, the better thing that Mary chose, is communion with Christ. Pure, sweet fellowship with our Lord and Saviour. Time spent quietly at the feet of Jesus.

Even in this lesson, in this rebuke, can you hear the tenderness, compassion and grace of Jesus? I urge you, precious child of God, to open your home to Him. Welcome Jesus into every nook and cranny. Don't keep any part of your life closed off. Be completely open and honest and real and you will enjoy a peace and an intimacy with Him like you have never known. He is oh so gracious and kind. Let's give Christ that rightful position of Lord over our lives! Today will you welcome Him in?

New Clothes

"I delight greatly in the LORD;
my soul rejoices in my God.
For He has clothed me with garments of salvation and
arrayed me in a robe of righteousness…"
~ Isaiah 61:10a, NIV ~

There is so much in this verse. So many parts and pieces of deep, rich truth. I could unpack it for days, and, as time goes on, I may just do that.

However, in this moment, I would like to share with you one specific truth that popped off the page of my Bible and into my heart. It is the way Isaiah says **_He_ has clothed me.** Did you catch it? God did it! He clothed me! He arrayed me. God Himself covered me with salvation and righteousness. God Himself, through Jesus Christ, made me right with Him! He alone saved me from sin and death!

Why is this a big deal? Because it shouts out the strongest reminder: I didn't do it! I *couldn't* do it. But the fact is, I tried. I spent years trying to cover myself, clean myself up, feel whole and pull myself out of the pit I was in. I was like Adam and Eve, grabbing every fig leaf I could find to hide my guilt and shame and sin, but no matter what I did, it didn't work. No matter how hard I tried, my righteousness was still as filthy rags. I couldn't change it.

No masks I wore, no kindnesses I showed, nothing could change who I was inside. No matter what I did or didn't do, I could not save myself.

Then one day I felt the Holy Spirit drawing me to Himself. I'd felt this gentle pull, this conviction, for some time, but I just ignored Him. Yet it seemed as though He was following me around with that free gift of salvation in His hand, holding that beautiful garment out to me. Offering it to me. But I kept refusing. Until finally one night I could refuse it no longer. I longed for that gift to be mine and I fell before my Jesus and cried out to Him. He took that old covering of sin off of me and replaced it with a glorious garment of salvation and robe of righteousness! I was now clothed in His spectacular grace! He washed me inside and out and I became a new creation!

Now, back then, I didn't know words like **righteousness**, but I didn't need to. I didn't need to know or to understand all the big, theological concepts; I just knew I was different. I knew I was not the same person and I never would be again. And I knew that God had done it! It was He Who had clothed me with salvation and wrapped me in His righteousness. *He* saved me. When I acknowledged my utter helplessness to change myself, change came. Through the finished work of Jesus Christ on the cross, God did what only he can do. He did for me what I could never do for myself.

So yes, I will praise Him! And if you have been made right with God, then praise Him, dear one! Take a moment to ponder what He has done for you and rejoice greatly in our God and Saviour!

I love the way The Message Bible says the first part of this verse: ***"I will sing for joy in God, explode in praise from deep in my soul...!"***

Healed and Helping

*"When Jesus came into Peter's house,
he saw his mother-in-law
lying in bed with a fever.
He touched her hand and the fever left her,
and she got up and began to wait on them."*
~ Matthew 8:14-15, NIV ~

This is one of my favorite miracles that Jesus performed. Being only two short verses, it is quite easy to read then move on past without giving it a second thought. In fact, I read it several times and didn't even see what and amazing message was sitting before me! Just two wee verses. Go ahead; read them again. Listen to their simplistic beauty.

Jesus went to Peter's house. Peter's mother-in-law was sick. Jesus healed her. Isn't that great? Jesus **touched her hand and the fever left her.** It's an amazing thing! But did you notice how verse fifteen ends? **And she got up and waited on them.**

In Luke's account of this miracle, he tells us that **she got up <u>at once</u> and began to wait on them.** (Luke 4:39) Other translations, such as the English Standard Version, use the word **serve**. She got up and served them. And do you know what the J. B. Phillips New Testament says? **And then she got up and began to <u>see their needs</u>**.

How cool is that?! As soon as Peter's mom-in-law was well, she saw the needs of those around her, and got right in to meeting those needs. What an amazing and convicting lesson!

You may think to yourself, *well, I've never been sick like that; I've never been healed that way.* No, not physically, perhaps, but if you know Christ as your Saviour, He has most certainly healed you. Ephesians 2:1 says **you were dead in your transgressions and sins.** Dead! You can't get any sicker than that! Verse five of Ephesians 2 goes on to say that **you were made alive with Christ**! Precious child of God, indeed you have been healed. And because of this truth, we, too, must see the needs of those around us and get up and serve. There is a place for you, and there is so much work to be done for the kingdom of God.

If you are not serving others in any way, please ask yourself: *Why not?* What is stopping you? Fear? Uncertainty? Feelings of inadequacy or unimportance? These, too, require Jesus's healing touch. When Mark told this story, he added a beautiful snippet of information. He tells us that **Jesus went to her, took her hand and helped her up.** (Mark 1:31) He will do the same for you. In faith, take hold of Jesus's hand. He will help you up. He will open the doors where you can serve Him, and He will give you all you need to serve Him well.

What's in Your Hand?

"Then the LORD said to him,
'What is that in your hand?'
'A staff', he replied."
~ Exodus 4:2, NIV ~

After murdering an Egyptian, Moses ran away from Pharoah, left Egypt, and came to the land of Midian (Ex. 2:11-22). There he settled down, married, and in Exodus 3:1, we read that Moses found a new job. He began tending his father-in-law's flocks. Moses became a shepherd. Like all shepherds, he carried a staff. It was an ordinary piece of equipment used to tend the sheep and goats. It was *his* staff.

But now God had a new job for Moses. In a way he will remain a shepherd, but rather than tending flocks of animals, leading them around the pastures, he will be leading God's people out of slavery and through the wilderness. The very wilderness he is standing in at this moment.

When it was time for this new job to begin, God called Moses from the burning bush, commissioning him to go back to Egypt and to command Pharoah to let His people go (Ex. 3). Moses was afraid and needed some reassurance. He was afraid that when he went back, Pharoah and the other Egyptians would not believe that God had appeared to him, and that they would not listen to what he had to say (Ex. 4:1). And that is where my verse comes in. When Moses talked with God about his fears, God asked him what he held in his hand, and Moses simply replied, *"A staff."*

God then used that staff to perform evidential miracles, signs that Moses would use in front of Pharoah when the time came for them to meet. Signs that would prove that it was for certain the LORD Who sent him there.

At the end of the burning bush conversation, in Exodus 4:17, as God sends Moses on his way, He reminds Him to take his staff, so that *"you can perform miraculous signs with it."* And that is exactly what Moses did. He went to Egypt. But listen to this. Look really closely as you read the verse that tells us about Moses's journey –

In Exodus 4:20, we are told that **Moses took his wife and sons, put them on a donkey and started back to Egypt. And he took the staff of God in his hand.** Did you catch it? It is now called **the staff of God**! This ordinary shepherd's tool, Moses's staff, now belonged to God, and would be used for His plans and purposes. Just a plain old stick wasn't just a plain old stick anymore. I find that incredible!

What this taught me, and continues to teach me, is that what I have in my hand can be used for God's plans and purposes if I give it to Him. It's His anyway, so just entrust Him with it all and watch what He will do! What do you and I have that is plain, ordinary, unimpressive even, that, when we give it to the LORD, can be used for service in the kingdom? We must never think that we don't have anything useful; that we ourselves could not be useful. Remember, God uses the most unlikely people and ordinary things to do His good work.

As for me, well, I have this laptop, so I will use if for His glory. What about you? Using the very words of our LORD, I must ask – ***"What is that in your hand?"***

Extraordinary Courage

*"When they saw the courage of Peter and John
and realized that they were unschooled,
ordinary men, they were astonished
and they took note that these men had been with Jesus."*
~ Acts 4:13, NIV ~

Peter and John stood before the Sanhedrin, waiting to be questioned. Why? Well, not only had they healed a crippled beggar, they had also been speaking to the people about Jesus. The Jewish leaders were particularly bothered by their teachings regarding the resurrection of the dead. And so, they were seized by the temple guard and put in jail for the night (Acts 4:1-3).

The following day, the boys were brought before the Jewish supreme court, presided over by the high priest, and were asked one of the greatest questions ever: ***"By what power or name do you do this?"*** (Acts 4:7b) And Peter answered. Boldly. Confidently. Unwavering and unapologetic, filled with the Holy Spirit, Peter answered. He stood before that formidable group of men and declared: ***"It is by the name of Jesus Christ of Nazareth."*** (Acts 4:10a).

As they listened, that ruling council of seventy-one men **were astonished**. They were amazed because of the courage Peter and John exhibited as they stood before the council, completely sure of themselves and unintimidated. How could they do that? How could they stand there, speaking so boldly, with such knowledge and insight? I mean, they knew where these boys had come from. They knew they were **unschooled, ordinary men**. They had not been to Rabbinical school. They had no formal training in theology. Yet they spoke as though they had the finest Jewish education. And in a sense, they did.

While it was true that Peter and John had not been to school, they **had been with Jesus**. Oh yes, these former fishermen received a better education than any of those men sitting in the courtroom that day. Peter and John had spent time with Jesus! They walked with Him for three years. They listened to and were taught by the greatest Teacher that ever lived. They watched their Master as He interacted with people and shared Himself with them. They had private lessons, face-to-face with the Son of God. And now they were filled with the Holy Spirit, and all that Jesus taught them while He was with them, they were able to proclaim with absolute confidence.

And the Sanhedrin was at a loss as to what to do with Peter and John. I mean, they didn't even argue with the answer Peter gave them regarding the man who was healed (Acts 4:8-12). They couldn't! And they certainly could not *deny* the healing. **Since they could see the man that had been healed standing there with them, there was nothing they could say** (Acts 4:14). How could they argue with such evidence? The Truth was in them and on their side.

And dear one, that is all that matters! It is of no concern that you are without fancy letters behind your name. Oh, please hear me, I am not down-playing those with a fine education, not at all! I say – good for you! I'm proud of you! And I pray that you are using your learning for the glory of God.

But at the same time, not everyone has a great deal of schooling, yet as you spend time with Jesus you will learn from Him. As you read your Bible it will transform you and train you. Jesus will give you knowledge and wisdom and boldness just as surely as He gave it to Peter and John so long ago. Remember, they were fisherman. Since they were involved in the family business, it is quite likely that, while they had some education, as all Jewish children did, they didn't go "all the way", as we might say. But that did not matter. Not to Jesus. All he asked them and us to do is to spend time with Him. To follow Him. To take His yoke upon us and learn from Him. He is the greatest Teacher Who ever lived. As you sit with Him and spend time in His presence, reading and studying His Word, you will be taught. And you, too, will learn to be courageous like Peter and John. You will be enabled to speak and to serve in whatever way He calls you.

~ ~ ~ ~ ~ ~ ~ ~ ~ ~ ~ ~

In the introduction of this book, I shared how it had become difficult for me to leave the house for work because of my growing passion to read and study the Bible. Well, I continued working in daycare for about another year, and throughout that time I read what I could in the mornings, carried my pocket verses with me through the day, then in the evening, after the kids were settled, I would sit down in what became known as "my spot" at the table and study my Bible. Night after night, week after week, month after month. I read and read and read.

One evening as I sat there, a crazy idea came to mind. Oh, it wasn't the first time I'd had this thought. Remember the mentor I mentioned in the introduction? Well, as I began sharing with her the verses and the things I learned, she confirmed what I had been thinking: I was to lead a women's Bible study. Yet it was an idea I quickly rejected each time it came up.

So that one night, the Bible study wrestling began again. May I pause here to tell you just how thankful I am for the kindness and gentleness and patience of our Lord?! The sweet Holy Spirit does not give up on us. No, he gently guides us and moves us along in our faith, leading us into these good works that He has prepared in advance for us to do (Eph. 2:10). I simply adore Him!

Anyway, back to that night. Back to my spot. Back to my wrestling. There I was, trying to brush that thought away like a pesky fly that wouldn't leave me alone. I talked to God, "explaining" to Him why this was not a good idea. And I proceeded to give God a very thorough and well-thought-list of why it would never work. Still too young in my faith. Too quiet. Too shy. Too scared...of so many things. And most of all, I had no fancy titles in front of my name or letters behind it. I was completely uneducated. *"How could I do it",* I asked God.

Then, as so often happens with the living Word of God, my eyes were drawn to His answer. It was this verse. It was Acts 4:13. I looked at those words and realized they fit me, too. I am unschooled. And I am definitely ordinary. But, like Peter and John, I had been with Jesus. For about two years I had sat with Him every single day, learning from Him. The Holy Spirit had been teaching me and training me and I hadn't even recognized it. He was pouring His truth into me, not just to keep for myself, but to share with others.

And so, in that moment I understood. I, too, have the Spirit living in me, and just as He gave Peter and John such wisdom to tell people about Jesus, He will do the same for me. In a very real sense, I didn't matter. God called me, and He will equip me. Who I was, where I came from, formal education or not, none of that counted. The thing that mattered most is that I had been with Jesus.

I did say yes to God that night, and he opened doors that I never thought possible. I have the privilege of writing lessons from the Bible and teaching the sweetest ladies you'd ever want to meet. One of my greatest joys in life is sitting with those ladies, studying our Bibles together, walking deeper into the grace and knowledge of our Lord Jesus Christ.

And if I may add just one more thing. I know for certain that what God did for me He will do for you. No, your service to Him may not look the same as mine, but according to the scriptures, we have all been called to proclaim the good news of Jesus Christ. And I further know that we need courage to do that. We need to be bold. We may very well face much opposition the way Peter and John did, so we need to be prepared.

I don't know what the Lord has for you, dear one, but I must encourage you to make time each day to be with Jesus. Take time to read and pray. Allow His Word to train you and equip you. And then, in the power of His Name, go forth and proclaim our glorious Saviour!

Calling Him Father

"Draw near to God and he will draw near to you."
~ James 4:8a, ESV ~

It is a very simple thing I want to share about this verse. A simple yet profound discovery.

When I first became a Christian, I always called God *God*. No surprise, eh? I mean, that's Who He is. So, any time I talked with Him, that is the name I used. But one day I noticed that not only did I call Him God, but I often began calling Him Father.

Father. A much more intimate name. A sweet and tender name. A close and connected name. And I began to wonder how that happened. And when?

As I pondered and prayed over this transition, the answer came quietly one day: it happened while I read my Bible. See, as we know, the Bible is the very heart of God. It is, quite literally, His written words. We get to know Him when we read it.

In those early days I didn't understand any of this. All I knew was, as I alluded to earlier, I felt the Holy Spirit drawing me to my Bible. Over and over, I would have this thought: *read the Word*. When I was obedient to that instruction, (finally), I was actually drawing nearer to God, and He was indeed drawing nearer to me. As I said, I didn't understand that's what was happening, but now, looking back, I know that it was. The more time I spent reading and talking to God about the stuff I was learning, the more I got to know Him. And the more I got to know Him, the closer I felt to Him. My love and trust for God was ever-increasing, and somewhere in those days, He became Father to me. I mean, He always is Father, but for me, as my relationship with God grew, I began to experience the reality of that. He was, is and always will be my loving Father.

This command from James is vitally important to obey. And it is a command! A loving and earnest command. And the promise within is absolutely certain to be kept. God *will* draw near to you. I can't tell you exactly how it will happen, but it will. There is something that the Spirit of God does when we lean into Him that causes us to know for certain that He is leaning back. And, although I am sure there are other ways of drawing near to God, such as praise and worship and prayer, I have learned that reading His Word is one of the sweetest ways. The reward we get in doing so is closeness and connectedness to God unlike anything we could imagine. Every moment we spend is a moment closer to Him, and it won't be long until we understand that He truly is our Father, our loving, helping, healing Father Who sincerely desires to be in close fellowship with you!

The Eternal Advocate

"And I will ask the Father,
and he will give you another advocate
to be with you forever –"
~ John 14:16, NIV ~

I had read these words of Jesus many times and have always been quite thrilled when I would "sit down" in that upper room with the disciples and imagine them hearing this teaching of Jesus for the first time. Jesus had just told His guys that He would be leaving, but that He would send **another advocate**. But one day, as I studied the verse more in depth, I was completely overjoyed with what it meant for me, and for all of us today.

See, I got to wondering what the word **advocate** really meant. I knew Jesus was telling us about the Holy Spirit, but I love going back to the original language to find out what it can teach me, and when I did, what I found was quite thrilling! I discovered in my Strong's Concordance that this Greek word, *paraklētos*, means *called to one's aid*. And Thayer's Lexicon describes it as *summoned; called to one's side to help*. I love that! This was huge to me! I can't tell you how my heart felt when I read it, other than to say it was filled with a kind of gratitude and relief that I hadn't felt before. I mean, I believed by faith that the Holy Spirit dwelt within me, and that He was doing His good work in me and for me, but to see it written this way, to better understand what was happening was delightful! Just listen to that: *called to one's side to help.*

That is what the Spirit is doing day by day, moment by moment. I immediately got this image of a worn and weary person, walking along, scarcely able to take another step, but then One most powerful comes along, wrapping a strong and loving arm around that person, enabling him or her to continue on. And together, they do just that. Together, they make it through. That is what it is like for me. And, as we clearly see in this verse, you and I have this blessed gift **forever**.

What was even more joyful was when I looked at several other Bibles, wanting to see how they translate the word *paraklētos*. I was excited to discover the words they use are **Comforter** (KJV), **Counselor**, (CJB) **Helper** (ESV), **Intercessor** (AMP, AMPC), **Strengthener** (AMP, AMPC), **Companion** (CEB), and **Friend** (MSG). What a beautiful and powerful list! How I praise God for Him! And if you are a child of God, you have this **Counselor**, who is the Holy Spirit, dwelling in you. And He is all these things for you.

So today, as you get up and begin to do all that God has called you to do, remember the Holy Spirit. Go forth in His power. Rely on Him. Depend on Him. Trust and believe that He is with you; that you are never alone! He will come alongside you and strengthen you. He will comfort you and fight for you. He is with you forever!

Waking Up Hungry

> *"I have treasured the words of his mouth*
> *more than my daily bread."*
> *~ Job 23:12b ~*

I love this verse. When I first read it, I decided that I want this proclamation to be true for me. This is the simple desire of my heart, that I would treasure God's Word more than my daily bread.

I want to desire His commands, His promises, all the words that God has breathed out in the Holy Scriptures. I want to store them up inside of me so that I can live by them, the way that Job, in his day, stored wheat and grain away to be kept safe from weather and looters. I long to wake up each morning for this spiritual food that will provide me with nourishment for my soul, tucking the goodness of the Word away into my heart and mind.

I fear, however, that all too often I wake up and go through my days hungry for other things. What you and I value is what we feast on and tuck away into secret places, and those aren't always the things that matter. I can tend to feast on worldly things and hunger for my own selfish delights.

So I pray and ask God to give me this desire of my heart. *"Please, Lord, help me to want the words of Your **mouth more than my daily bread**."*

In the early days of my walk with God, that is what came to mind as I pulled this wee verse from my pocket and pondered it. It became a prayer, one I realized that God was indeed answering! With each pocket verse that I studied and internalized, His Word was being stored away, treasured up in my heart. I am so very grateful for the good work that He has done and is doing within me and it thrills me to know that He will do the same for you!

~ ~ ~ ~ ~ ~ ~ ~ ~ ~ ~ ~ ~

Those were my initial thoughts on this verse from Job, and they are still true. I still long to treasure God's Word most. But tonight, so many years after I first discovered and wrote about it, as I type this wee devotional, something else comes to mind – the context in which Job wrote these words –

Eliphaz, a friend of Jobs, came to be with him in his time of deep, deep despair. Job had suffered loss and illness unlike anything like we could even imagine. It brought him to emotional and physical devastation, and the friends who came did little to provide true comfort. That included Eliphaz.

This guy was accusing Job of great wickedness, therefore arousing God to anger so that He poured out His wrath upon Job. Eliphaz is trying to get Job to repent, to turn back to the LORD and His ways, and in his wrongful accusations and pleading he says to Job: ***"Accept instructions from his mouth and lay up his words in your heart."***, (Job 22:22, NIV). Then here, in Job 23:12, Job in effect responds, *"I am! I have treasured up His word! I've* *treasured it more than my necessary food! I am accepting instruction from God!"*

Do you see how wonderful this is? This isn't a bragging moment from Job. It doesn't even seem to be even a case of self-defense. Job is simply speaking the truth about his relationship with God. He is telling Eliphaz the facts about where is heart and his behaviors were before all this mess began. And do you know what that means? Do you know what this reminds me of once again? That even if you are living like Job, living with an intense yearning to know God more and to live by His commands and to love Him most, life can still be filled with difficulty and tragedy and grief!

Have you ever found yourself crying out, *"Why me? What have I done? Why am I being punished? I've been following You, Jesus! I've been doing what You call me to do!"* Have you ever found yourself being your own Eliphaz? Well, there's nothing wrong with searching your heart for unconfessed sin; that is a right and proper thing to do. The scriptures encourage such self-reflection. But just because every time you pick up the telephone there is more bad news, that does *not* mean God is punishing you! That's what Job's friends were assuming; that it was all his fault. That was the whole basis for their "encouragement".

But Eliphaz was wrong. The other guys were wrong, too. So very wrong. In describing Job, God Himself said that **"there is no one on earth like him; he is blameless and upright, a man who fears God and shuns evil."**, (Job 1:8b, NIV). Can you imagine? There could be no better commendation! So, unconfessed sin was not an issue in this wreckage of Job's life! Not treasuring God's Word was *not* the issue!

Why then? Why did Job suffer so? And why do we suffer in ways that seem perplexing and even unfair? Well, here's my answer: I don't know. I just don't always know. We live in a broken, fallen, sinful world where bad things happen and none of us are exempt. And I am very sorry for whatever it is you are going through right now.

What I do know, however, with absolute certainty, is that God knows! Our Father understands *exactly* what is happening to you and me, just like He did with Job. And he knows why. And He knows for how long and what will be accomplished through it. There was a greater purpose in that suffering, and, as with Job, there is purpose in our suffering and losses as well. Purpose that may or may not become clear over time. Purpose that we can trust God with, even when we cannot understand it.

Oh, I do hope this brings some comfort right now! If you are in the midst of the pain or the depths of despair, you desperately want answer and I get that. I do. But here in this moment, cling to what you know to be true: that God is good. ***"He is the Rock, his works are perfect, and all His ways are just. A faithful God who does no wrong, upright and just is he."*** (Deut. 32:4, NIV) It is that truth which leads me back to where I started –

No matter what the situation you find yourself in, keep treasuring the Word of God. Hold fast to its truths. Allow the Holy Spirit to comfort you as you read. Learn and grow and live in light of the Word. Let it be the healing balm that your heart needs. And if I may, I'd like to give you a place to look into regarding this subject, with Job specifically, although there are so, so many others. Take some time to reflect on James 5:10-11. Then go back to Job. Read the end of his account, Job 42:1-16, and see what came from his perseverance.

Then...

> *"Then I will teach transgressors Your ways,*
> *so that sinners will turn back to You."*
> *~ Psalm 51:13, NIV ~*

Psalm 51 is a fairly well-known Psalm. In these verses we hear King David cry out to the LORD in repentance after he committed adultery with Bathsheba and arranged the murder of her husband.

As I was reading through this Psalm one day, verse thirteen hit me in a really big way. I hadn't noticed it before, but suddenly that day, I heard the words within the whole context, and the beauty of it jumped off the page of my Bible. I'll show you what I mean. Let's take a quick walk through David's prayer --

David begins by crying out to God for **mercy, according to** His **unfailing love** and **great compassion**. He acknowledges his sin and guilt, and pleads with God to **cleanse** him so he can **be clean**, to **wash** him so he can **be whiter than snow**. David passionately requests that the LORD **blot out** all his **iniquities** and **create in** him a **pure heart**. Finally, David seeks restoration. He says in verse twelve: **Restore to me the joy of your salvation and grant me a willing spirit, to sustain me.** The Living Bible simply says **make me willing to obey you.** I love that!

And then comes the verse that I hadn't really noticed before. I certainly hadn't made the connection. So – after David repents and finds forgiveness, after he is purified and restored to a right relationship with God, he says, -- **"Then"** …

And there you have the connecting word! Then. Then what, you may ask? Well, look at the verse again, verse thirteen. ***"Then I will teach transgressors your ways, so that sinners will turn back to you."*** Is that amazing or what?! No experience wasted. After he goes from rock-bottom sinfulness to the joy and freedom of confession and wholeness, then he will teach other transgressors the ways of God. How beautiful is that?!

David knew how quickly temptation led to sin and that one sin led to another. He then knew very well the chastening hand of God and the torment of guilt and unconfessed sin. But when he fell before the LORD in true repentance, he was met with true grace and forgiveness. Those are God's ways. Grace and forgiveness. That is what David could now teach others who are sinning against God. He will teach others the reality of sin and the bitter consequences that will surely follow. He will use his experiences to help others come to that place of repentance, to testify of the amazing power of God's love and mercy! David understood that in both discipline and in forgiveness, God shows His extraordinary grace! He felt the cleansing power of God, and now, he will share this good news with others.

So I'm wondering, now that you are forgiven, what will you do with the good news? What will I do? Who will we teach? Remember, teaching in this sense does

Then...

not involve higher education and degrees. No, this kind of teaching involves love for the Lord and for the people He places in our lives. It's about extreme gratitude for a life that has been changed by the forgiveness of sin! David no doubt simply shared his story. He gave testimony to how God restored his life and we can do the same. David cried, **"Cleanse me with hyssop, and I will be clean; wash me and I will be whiter than snow"** (Ps. 51:7, NIV). We have been made clean, washed by the very blood of Jesus! We definitely have something to teach!

One last thing that comes to mind: David didn't teach others until he himself was right with the LORD. If there is any sin that you are living in and have not repented of, please do that now. Confess it, and you will surely find forgiveness! You will be cleansed and restored! Then you, too, will have a story to teach others. You can teach them the loving, merciful, gracious ways of God!

**To read this portion of David's story, scoot back to 2 Samuel, and read chapters eleven and twelve.

One Thing I Know

"He replied,
'Whether he is a sinner or not, I don't know.
One thing I do know.
I was blind but now I see!'"
~ John 9:25, NIV ~

If there is one thing I admire about this unnamed man, it is that he had the courage, the wisdom and the humility to say, *"I do not know."* And with the same courage, and with conviction, he declared that which he knew for certain –

The man in the story has been born without sight. He's been in the dark his whole life, and now he lives as a beggar just to survive. He was born blind, we are told, so that God's glorious works could **be displayed in him** (John 9:3b). And the day Jesus walked by and saw the man, that is exactly what happened. The blind man had an encounter with the Healer, he was healed, and for certain, God's amazing works were illustrated through him! For the first time in his life, the beggar could see!

Everyone took notice of this miracle, and then the questions began. Questions and accusations. The man's neighbors were the first to notice and inquire not only into the healing itself, but also if he was indeed the actual man who used to sit begging. They, in turn, took him to the Pharisees, and the questions extended out to wondering about the one who had performed the miracle, and who did it on the Sabbath!

Soon his parents were brought in and the inquisition continued. They affirmed that yes, he was their son, and for sure he had been born blind, but they would not speak on their son's behalf regarding the miracle that had taken place. They directed the questions back to their son because, they said, he is old enough to **speak for himself** (John 9:18-21). And speak he did! Over and over, he told the brief story of how **the man they call Jesus** had healed him (John 9:11)

But, as is so often the case, the Pharisees were just not having it. In their unbelief they would not take *miracle* for an answer. And for certain they would not accept Jesus as the Healer! So – **"A second time they summoned the man who had been blind. 'Give glory to God by telling the truth', they said. 'We know this man is a sinner'"** (John 9:9:24). They were accusing Jesus of being a sinner, therefore unable to perform such miracles.

And this is where my verse comes in. The healed man did not know whether or not Jesus was a sinner. He didn't actually know Jesus at all. Afterall, the two had only met briefly, and when that interaction happened, the man was still blind! But what he did know with certainty, as he declared so boldly, **"I was blind but now I see!"**

As a new believer in Christ, this verse spoke very powerfully to me. I learned two very valuable lessons from this unnamed man and the words he spoke.

First, I learned that it is perfectly fine not to have all the answers. It's okay to say, as the blind man did, *I*

do not know when someone asks you a question about Jesus, or if they ask you the difficult questions about our faith in Christ and about our God. It's good to have the same honesty as this man. The same courage, wisdom, and humility. We don't have to have all the answers when we talk to people. In fact, we *can't* have all the answers. Although over time we will grow in knowledge and wisdom, I don't think we will ever fully comprehend Jesus and His ways. That is especially true when we are new believers. As I said, when I first read this verse, I had only known Jesus a short while. I didn't get all the theology and doctrine about salvation. I didn't understand exactly Who Jesus is and what He accomplished on that cross, but somehow, by the work of the Holy Spirit, I knew He died for me. Nope, I sure couldn't answer the big questions at that time, but there was something I could tell people –

The blind man did not stop with what he did *not* know; he went on to tell the Pharisees and the crowd of people what he *did* know. I love how he stood in front of those doubters and accusers and curious ones and declared, **"One thing I do know. I was blind but now I see!"** That is awesome! That is what I, too, am able to declare! And so can you! That story is the same for all of us who have placed our faith in the Lord Jesus Christ. All we who have had an encounter with Christ have had our spiritual eyes opened. We were blind to the truth of our sinfulness and our need of a Saviour. Our eyes were veiled to the truth of the gospel, but now they have been opened and we can see!

No, we may not have every answer, but we do have a testimony. And no one can refute what Jesus has done for us! No one! So tell them, child of God! Declare to all what Jesus has done for you!

Leading the Way

*"After three days the officers went throughout the camp,
giving orders to the people:
'When you see the ark of the covenant
of the LORD your God,
and the Levitical priests carrying it,
you are to move out from your positions and follow it.
Then you will know which way to go, since you have
never been this way before.'"*
~ Joshua 3:2-4a, NIV ~

Several years ago, I was going through a really difficult situation. An unexpected situation. I had never experienced anything like it before and I was scared. I felt so lost and didn't know which way to turn.

That evening as I sat reading my Bible and praying, my eyes became fixed on this particular sentence: **"Then you will know which way to go, since you have never been this way before."** I cried out to the LORD, *"I have never been this way before, Father! What do I do? How do I make it through?"* This place I found myself in was such new territory, but here God's Word told me **"THEN you will know which way to go --"** *When and how will I know*, I wondered. My eyes desperately scanned the previous verses. The answer had to be in there, and sure enough, it was.

The Ark of the Covenant of the LORD represents God's very presence. The Israelites, with Joshua leading them, were about to cross the Jordan into the Promised Land. They would be travelling through a land they had never seen, facing enemies they had never faced. They would be dealing with both battles and blessings they had never known. And they had to cross this raging river, an obstacle that seemed insurmountable. So Joshua's military officers told the Israelites that when they see the Ark move, they were to get up and follow it. I like the way the NASB says, ***"go after it"***! They were to stay in God's presence! They were to follow Him because He would see them safely through.

It was the same for me the evening God first showed me this verse. He knew long before I cried out to Him the place I would be traveling through. He knew I had never been this way before; that I was facing a situation I had never faced. What, then, did our heavenly Father tell me to do? Through this verse He simply said, *"Stay with Me."*

Every day is a new day, and we never know what we might be facing. We have no idea what the next seconds may bring, let alone the next days and weeks and months. But what I do know, precious child of God, is that our lives will be full of "never been this way before". Good things and bad things. Battles and blessings. The birth of a baby, the death of a loved one. Weddings, divorces. Promotions and pink slips. Rebellious children and reconciliations. The list goes on and on. They are a constant in our lives, and they will continue to be. Oh, how easy it is to get lost during these times. We can so quickly lose our way if we try to make it through that unfamiliar place on our own.

In these beautiful verses God reminds us that we don't have to go alone. He says, in effect, *"when you see Me move, you move with Me."* Stay in His presence and He will help you. He will guide you. He will show you the way. Whenever you find yourself in a foreign land, you will always know which way to go when you follow the Sovereign Lord! **"For this God is our God forever and ever; He will be our guide even to the end!"** (Ps. 48:14, NIV). Thank You, Jesus!

The Difference

*"Then you will know which way to go,
since you have never been this way before.
But keep a distance of about two thousand cubits
between you and the ark; do not go near it."*
~ Joshua 3:4, NIV ~

Quite some time has passed since I wrote about the first part of this verse, but then, all these months later, I am drawn back to it once again. Only this time it is for a different reason.

As I sit here today, meandering through this passage, I once again find myself in a "never-been-this-way-before" situation. And, once again, I trust that this truth still stands: God will lead and I will follow. He will show me the way through. And in pondering such goodness, I am suddenly, acutely aware of the richness of the blessing that you and me have, that the Israelites did not have, a blessing that we find at the end of this verse.

As Joshua's military officers went throughout the camp instructing the Israelites as to how and when they would move forward across the Jordan River and into the Promised Land, not only did he tell them that they are to follow the Ark of the Covenant of the LORD that was being carried by the priests, they also gave another very specific and important rule: ***"But keep a distance***

of about two thousand cubits between you and the ark; do not go near it."

Two thousand cubits! In modern measurements, that is about three thousand feet. One thousand yards. That's almost half a mile! And in telling them not to go near the Ark, they were, in effect, reminding the people that they could not go near the presence of God!

Now, part of the reason for this rule may be logistical. I mean, practically speaking, if they all shoved and crowded around the Ark, it would be very difficult to follow. At least, that's how I see it as I picture this scene in my mind. Besides with the vast number of people, it was impossible to all get close anyway. But there's more to it than that.

As a rule, no one was ever to go near the Ark of the Covenant except those specifically in charge of carrying it, those ordered by God Himself (Num. 4:4-6, 15). Also, once the Tabernacle was set up and the Ark was placed in the Holy of Holies, only the High Priest could go in there, and that only once a year to make atonement for Israel (Lev. 16). To come near it any other time, any other way, for any other person, would mean certain death.

Think about it. What if it were the same today? Imagine if you were about to go a way you had never experienced before. Enemies to face. Battles to fight. A whole new land; a whole new experience. There would be fear and anxiety and uncertainty to overcome. There would be a possibility of getting lost. Now imagine if you heard someone calling out, *"Make sure you follow the LORD but don't get too close! You can only follow Him from a distance; you cannot come into the presence of God!"* It makes my heart desperately sad just thinking about it.

However, it also causes my heart to rejoice! Somewhere in the midst of the sadness and uncertainty of this new road I am traveling today, there is joy! I guess that is why this verse has been on my mind: to stir up that joy and to give me some perspective and focus. Because unlike those Israelites so long ago, in the midst of our ***never been this way before***, we are not only encouraged, we are *commanded* to **come near to God**! That's what James tells us in his book, specifically in James 4:8, NIV. And in that same verse, we are promised that when we do, **he**, God, **will come near to you**.

Do you hear the bigness and the coziness of that? And we are allowed, enabled to obey James's words, according to Hebrews 7:19, ESV, because of **a better hope...through which we draw near to God**! That better hope is, of course, our Jesus! Because of Him and through Him, we will never be told to stay away from God! Once we belong to Him, there will never be a moment when we cannot and will not be with Him and He with us! No, in fact, we are highly encouraged, and yes, even commanded to **approach God's throne with confidence, so that we may receive mercy and find grace to help us in our time of need** (Heb. 4:16, NIV) That's the difference the cross made for you and me! Jesus made all the difference!

I don't know what you are in the middle of right now. It might be something you've never, ever gone through before, nor ever expected to. But take heart, dear one, our God is here! He is near! You may have never been this way before, but He has, and He is already there, ready, willing and able to help you and guide you the whole way through. He will be with you every moment. So come near to Him with everything you have. Don't turn away from Him. Rest in Him and feel His comforting, mighty arms around you. Hunker down and gratefully bask in the presence of God, your all-knowing, ever-loving, ever-present Father. And keep your eyes fixed on Jesus, the one Who made it possible.

Delightful Counselors

"Your statutes are my delight; they are my counselors."
~ Psalm 119:24, NIV ~

The statutes of God are simply referring to the whole, written word of God and the everlasting, unchangeable authority of that word.

For the writer of Psalm 119, one who remains unknown for certain, they are words that he has taken delight in. He found pleasure and joy in what God has to say because His words have been so helpful to him. They have, in fact, become his counselors.

I'm honestly not sure of everything that was going on in this man's life. There is, however, a clue in the verse prior to this one that tells us at least one thing. In Psalm 119:23, ESV, we hear him say: ***"Even though princes sit plotting against me, your servant will meditate on your statutes."*** I love the way The Message says it: **"While bad neighbors maliciously gossip about me, I am absorbed in pondering your wise counsel."** I love that!

So we know that there were men talking hatefully against this guy, and surely their behavior would have brought him much hurt, disappointment or even anger. Maybe all three! Yet even so, his focus was not on the words spoken, rather, it was on the words written! He made a choice to meditate not on the bad neighbors, but on God's statutes! He studies and ponders and spends time thinking about the Word of God. In the midst of the trials, his mind is fixed on God's will and His ways, and that has obviously had an impact on his mind and heart. That is why he is able to say ***Your statutes are my delight; they are my counselors.***

When difficult times surround you, and all kinds of emotions flare up, you've got to know how to respond. You need someone who understands and can give you wisdom and answers and perspective. You need comfort and guidance and strength. You need truth! And all of that is found in God's statutes.

I have found this to be so true in my own life. I have discovered the joy and delight that these precious words bring to me in times of distress. All of these things I have mentioned here I have been given in times when I've needed them most. And yes, for certain God gives human counselors, as well as godly friends and pastors and such, and they are of great value to us. In fact, that's the way the Lord designed it to be – that we help one another. And I have been abundantly blessed with some of the most precious confidants. But even that help is most helpful when it is grounded in truths of the Scriptures.

There is no greater counsel than the Word of God. In light of that, I encourage you, dear one, to do as the psalmist does. Don't focus on all the critical and hateful words out there, instead, meditate on God's wisdom. Make what the LORD says the delight of your heart. Let His word counsel you through all your days.

A Light in the Dark

*"Your word is a lamp for my feet,
a light on my path."
~ Psalm 119:105 ~*

Years ago, my kids and I were once again on our way home from visiting family. It was late at night when I turned onto a country road that one of my boys didn't recognize. He wasn't familiar with the way I had chosen, and it made him a little nervous.

We drove along in the dark for a while, and my son was getting more and more distressed. I reminded him of all the other trips we had taken together, and that he could trust mama to get us all safely home. But then God gave me a more tangible idea.

I handed my daughter my cell phone, had her go to my maps and locate "home". After she got the direction going, she gave it to my son so he could hold the phone and watch exactly where we were driving. He could see for himself that not only were we on the right road and going in the right direction, but that for certain we were getting closer and closer to home. It was only then that he began to settle back in his seat and relax. His wee heart and mind were at ease and the rest of the trip was peaceful and fun. He sat there beside me in the dark with his hands and eyes fixed on that softly glowing map.

As I recall this story, I also recall this oh-so-familiar verse. It's like a warm blanket to me. This is a verse that we must not take advantage of, that is, we must not blow over it because of its "popularity". Afterall, we memorize it and quote it, we paint it on coffee mugs and embroider it on tea towels. But do we see it? Do we know it and believe it and do it? God's Word, the Bible, is a lamp for our feet and a light on our path. It illuminates our way, no matter how dark the way may be.

I'm quite certain every one of us knows what it is like to physically walk through the dark. And I am equally certain that we have experienced walking through dark places emotionally, spiritually, and relationally. Those seasons of darkness can leave us just as disoriented and distressed as my son was that night. They leave us wondering if we are on the right road at all and if we will be completely lost in the midst of it all. My answer to you is, no, we will make our way through because we have this assurance from God.

Our Bibles are filled with promises of guidance and direction and encouragement. The words teach us and lead us and give us the wisdom we need. They shine the light on our circumstances and make the way clear. In fact, listen to another verse in this same Psalm. In verse 130 it is written: ***The unfolding of your words gives light; it imparts understanding to the simple*** (NIV). Don't you love that?! And I love the way the Complete Jewish Bible says, ***Your words are a doorway that lets in light.*** That is so good!

That is exactly what God's Word has done for me over the years -- and will do for all of us if we let it in. Which, by the way, is a very necessary component to this. The promise of Psalm 119:105 stands firm, but we must open our Bibles with an expectant, teachable heart, asking the Holy Spirit to give us understanding. Only then can it illuminate our way, one step at a time. Only then will it be ***a lamp for*** our ***feet*** and ***a light on*** our ***path***. It will lead us through every dark and uncertain time. It will, in fact, lead us all the way home!

You know, I think back to that night driving along in the dark. My phone had been sitting in the cup holder, turned off. I had to turn it on. We had to open up that app and use it. And I remember looking over at my son as he held my phone close, staring intently at the map and listening to the directions. Although it was very dark, the phone gave off a wee glow of light. And in that wee glow, I saw peace in my son's face. He was no longer fearing or fretting.

How much more beautiful is the light of the Word of God? How much more does its' truths shine in the dark and lead the way for you and I? How much more will it light our way as we travel home?

Because They Trust

*"They were helped in fighting them,
and God delivered the Hagrites
and all their allies into their hands,
because they cried out to him during the battle.
He answered their prayers,
because they trusted in him."*
~ 1 Chronicles 5:20, NIV ~

The first chapters of 1 Chronicles are somewhat challenging, filled with long lists of genealogy, lists of only semi-pronounceable names. Quite honestly, the reading can get tedious as the writer goes on and on with those names, as well as an occasional battle story.

Even though that may be, it is important to read it anyway. It is good to spend time reading the whole Bible. I believe that. For so many reasons. One reason is that, if you don't, you are going to walk right past hidden treasures that can only be found when you are willing to dig. Yes, every now and then, as you work your way through what may be considered "less-than-exciting" places, you will come across a beautiful jewel that you would have missed if you just hurried past. This verse is an exact example of that, and I want to look at it carefully, like studying a diamond. So let's begin –

The first word is **they**, and it refers to the **Reubenites, the Gadites and the half-tribe of Manasseh** (v. 18). These two-and-a-half tribes **waged war against the Hagrites, Jetur, Naphish and Nobad** (v. 19). And you see in our verse today, the Israelites **were helped** in fighting against this vast army. Helped by whom? By God. Why did God help them? **Because they cried out to him during the battle.**

How simplistically beautiful is that? God's people called on Him during this difficult war and He heard and He was there. He helped them to overcome and to win! 'Cause that's what God does when His people call to Him. Do you see what a gem this is? But wait, there's more!

The Reubenites, the Gadites and the half-tribe of Mannaseh were a mighty force in and of themselves. How do I know that? Well, God told me! In verse eighteen of this chapter, we hear that these tribes of Israel **had valiant fighting men who carried shield and sword, who drew the bow, expert in war, 44,760, able to go to war** (v. 18, ESV). And go to war they did! They went after that enemy, but as we see, the amazing thing is, they did not attempt to win this battle in their own strength. I'm sure they could have. I mean, just look at verse eighteen again. They were equipped. They were trained. They were mighty. Yet they didn't say, "*We've got this!*" No, they did not trust in themselves, their training or their equipment, rather, they put their trust where it was supposed to be: in the LORD!

Once again, pause and see the wonder of it all. Pan out and see it in the midst of the bigger picture. This gem, this precious jewel sits here on the page of my Bible among so many names and statistics. It would be so easy to just walk by and miss it. Yet here it is, shining with an awesome example of Who God is and what he will do for those who call on Him! It is a glowing reminder that we must learn from and follow. When you are in the battle, cry out to God! And when you cry out to Him, pray with faith, knowing and believing that He will hear and act on behalf of His children. Trust Him to hear you and to help you. Rely on God alone for the win, no matter what battle you are in right now. Yes, use all the weapons he has given you, but trust in God. What a mighty God He is!

You know what? I want this in my life. I want to be like the Reubenites, Gadites and half-tribe of Mannaseh. If my story could be written, I want to live in such a way that it could say this: *He answered her prayers because she trusted in Him.* How or when God will answer, I don't know. But answer He will, and for certain, we will be victorious! I trust Him for that. For the glory of His Name!

Into His Ears

> *"In my distress I called upon the LORD;*
> *I cried to my God for help.*
> *From His temple he heard my voice;*
> *my cry came before him into his ears."*
> *~ Psalm 18:6 ~*

This is a psalm of David. In the introduction we are told that he sang this song to the LORD **on the day when the LORD rescued him from the hand of all his enemies, and from the hand of Saul** (ESV).

That's pretty intense! Having spent much time reading the accounts of Saul and other enemies that David faced, this is indeed a powerful verse! It taught me so many lessons, but one day as I read it, one particular thing caught my attention. One very sweet thing –

I absolutely love the way David says that when he cried out to God for help, not only was he completely confident that God heard his voice, *his* very own voice among a bazillion other voices, but he says that his cry **came before him, <u>into his ears</u>**! And those are the specific words that hit me. Because how precious is that? How intimate and kind. Seriously, when I first read this, I was taken aback at the closeness of this picture. In my minds' eye I got this image of two best friends, sitting together on a cozy couch, whispering quietly to one another. That's the picture that came to mind, and it amazed me because this is *God* David is talking about! God! The Holy One! The all-powerful Creator of the universe! **The LORD**, David calls Him. This is God's personal name. Personal, indeed! David's cry came up to *Him*, into His very ears. Like the secret whisper of a best friend, so it was heard.

As I pondered this truth, it warmed my heart and gave me even more confidence in and closeness with my LORD. I know that when I call Him for help, *I know* He hears my voice! I know that my cry reaches Him, all the way to Him like a desperate whisper. Just think about that. All the way to God's heavenly throne. Past the din of all the earth, past millions of other voices and unnumerable sounds. Through the heavens, down the streets of gold, into the inner sanctuary to the throne where God sovereignly rules in inapproachable light, a place too dazzling and beautiful to comprehend, in there, my cry for help is heard. Over the angelic choirs, through the singing of the seraphim who continually call out, **Holy, holy, holy, is the LORD God Almighty!** (Isa. 6:3), comes the sound of me. *Me!* 'Cause I'm His girl. And so are you. You are His girl or guy. His child. It is not in vain that we cry out to our great God and Father, no, not in vain at all. Are you not left speechless when you think of such wonder?!

God hears. God cares. It matters not how far away heaven and God Himself may seem, He is not far at all. No, dear child of God, be assured, He is only a whisper away.

Morning Words

"Let the morning bring me word of your unfailing love,
for I have put my trust in you."
~ Psalm 143:8a, NIV ~

Do you ever question God's love for you? Ever wonder if it's really real? Or maybe just need to be assured of that love? I do. Not nearly so much as I used to, but I have to admit that still, from time to time, I feel like a wee child standing before my Father asking Him, *"Do you love me?"*

In those moments I feel like David, pleading with God to give him a word about His love, some sort of reminder. I don't know if this is literal morning David speaks of or whether it is a metaphor for the end of a really dark time. Either way, David needs to know. *Let me hear about Your love, Lord!*

Maybe David was asking to feel it deeper. Maybe he was asking God to show it in a special way, to give some sort of tangible sign that His love was real and it was still there because circumstances surely didn't seem to reflect that love. He needed to know because it was God alone that he trusted. And so, David ran to the LORD for comfort and reassurance.

There was a day when I came upon this verse that I was feeling very much like David. That old insecurity began creeping in again. I mean, I knew God loved me. The evidence is all around me. All I have to do is look to the cross and I know. He sent His one and only Son to die in my place. He sent Jesus, through Whom I am able to have a relationship with Him. This is, in fact, the greatest form of this lovingkindness of God. And I had experienced His love so many personal ways before. Yet on this particular morning, I found myself praying this verse, asking God for a reminder. *"Let this morning bring me word"*, I sighed. Circumstances were not good, and I just needed to know that my Father truly still cared, and that I could still trust in His love.

Later that morning, I was walking from my car into the grocery store, and as I walked, I continued to whisper, *"Lord, I know You love me, but I just need to know some more. Will you tell me that You love me?"*

Suddenly, from across the parking lot, I heard a voice call my name. I looked over and recognized that it was a sweet elderly couple that I know. They were sitting in their truck looking over their shopping list before they went inside. I went over to say hi to them, and when I got there, the man reached his hand out through the window, took my hand in his and said to me, *"We saw you and called you over because we wanted to tell you that we love you!"*

I was truly stunned! It was as though those words were coming straight from God Himself. The morning had indeed brought me word of His unfailing love, and I didn't even try to hold back the tears that slipped from my heart in that moment. The man's wife had now joined her hands with ours, and we held fast to one another and

I told them that I loved them too. And I told them how they had been used by God in a powerful and very tender way that morning. With joyful hearts we praised the Lord together in that parking lot. We praised Him for His unfailing love. And of course, I thanked my Father for an answer to prayer that only He could have orchestrated!

This might be a morning, a moment of any time of day, that finds you wondering, questioning, needing a little reassurance about the love of God. If it is, may I be the one to call you over and say, *"Yeah, He love you. Absolutely He does. No matter what your world looks like right now, Jesus is living proof of that love!"* I pray that you will trust in it this whole day through. And when you get a moment, will you please take some time to read this whole Psalm? Listen to the plea of David's heart in its' fullness. Allow God's very own word to bring that comfort and confidence to your own heart today.

~ ~ ~ ~ ~ ~ ~ ~ ~ ~ ~ ~ ~

It's been several years since I first wrote the words of that story, and as I am re-writing them for this book, I realized there's something I'd like to add. It's important because since that time, I have learned much more about the **unfailing love** that David was praying about.

The Hebrew word for this phrase is *ḥesed*. It is a deeply rich and full Hebrew word, and there's really no English word that will encompass its entire meaning. However, after studying many books, one thing I learned is that this love, *ḥesed*, is not simply a feeling or an emotion. It is a deep and loving commitment that causes God to step in and help those in need, to move and to act on behalf of people. It is about God's kindness and mercy; His faithfulness and His attentiveness to His children. It is not earned by us; there is nothing we can do to deserve it. It is Who God is. It is limitless love, generous and devoted. The English Standard Version used the term **steadfast love**, and the New English Translation calls is **loyal love.**

So, what I am getting at is this: David was crying out for God's *ḥesed*. He didn't only need a word about God's love in the sense of a warm, fuzzy feeling, no, it was so much more than that. David needed a reminder of just how loyal God is! He needed to know that God, in His great compassion, would show up; that He cared enough to do something and that He was still there in the midst of the darkness. And as you read the Psalm in its entirety, you will hear what it is that David longs for God to do.

That morning so long ago, as I cried out to God, in His compassion and kindness, He did indeed show up. He came because He cared. I've never had an experience quite like that again, but I will treasure it always. And as thankful as I am for that moment, I've got something even better. I've got Jesus. My Saviour. My most loyal and faithful Friend. My Redeemer. Jesus, Who showed up with the greatest love and compassion. By faith and by evidence, I know and believe that yes, Jesus loves me!

Fear and Faith

"When I am afraid, I put my trust in You."
~ Psalm 56:3a ~

Fear has always been a part of my life to one degree or another. I don't easily use the word *always*, but in this case, sadly, it accurately applies.

That is why I love the succinctness of this verse. I love the honestly and the clarity and the directness. David, the writer of the Psalm, says, **<u>when</u> I am afraid**. Right up front he acknowledges that yes, he does get scared. David, the great warrior, the future king of Israel, is frightened. Fear is a very real response, especially in some of the situations David found himself, and I appreciate not only his honesty, but also his humility in confessing those feelings. After all, admitting it is the first step in doing something about it, right?

So what do you do when you get scared, David? Well, he simply says, ***I put my trust in you.*** Period. He is speaking of God, of course. I see in there that it is an action that David takes. ***I put.*** It is a conscious decision. Something thought-out, intentional, decisive. It is a choice that he makes. He puts his trust in the LORD.

The fact is that we all trust in something. Every one of us puts our confidence somewhere or in someone. Just think about it a moment. When fear and anxiety creep in, what's the first thing you think about? To whom or to what do you and I immediately run to? That's a pretty good indication of where our trust lies.

And furthermore, the truth is that we all get scared from time to time. Let's be honest, as David was. It's okay to take a moment and recognize that yeah, I'm kinda freaked out right now. My anxiety level is definitely rising. Fear is a normal response to many things. It's not a matter of *if* it will happen, but *when*. But we know and understand that God does not want us to be afraid. He has not given us the spirit of fear (1 Tim. 1:7), but knowing it will come, He gives us the remedy. And David knew exactly what that remedy was. Or might I say, *Who* it is!

The remedy, of course, is God Himself! The ever-present, all-wise God of peace and comfort. David makes that very clear. And I am learning more and more to use David's words, to make the choice he made. When I feel fear, I say something like this: *"Okay, God, I'm really scared, but I'm gonna put my trust in You."* And I begin talking to Him about the specifics of why I am afraid, of exactly what situation has prompted it. I talk to Him, out loud, if possible, and I ask Him, *"What does trusting You look like in this moment? Does it mean doing something? Or simply waiting on You?"* And I speak truth about what I know about God, Who He is, what He has done for me in the past, and what I know He can do in the present and in the future. My faith in Him grows, and it isn't long until the fear begins to melt away.

There are a couple of things I encourage you to do. First, as always, read this whole Psalm. Get the full context and beauty. When you do, you will see that, according to the introductory heading, it is *a miktam of David, when the Philistines seized him at Gath*, (ESV).

Second, it would be good to read that story, too, which you will find in 1 Samuel 21:10 -15. In it you will find two specific moments in David's life, one that brought him to this place of trust that he is in when he writes this psalm, and another that caused him to act, well, a little crazy. You will see that David did not trust in God perfectly, rather, he did it progressively, just as you and I do. You will see that at some point, David pulled himself away from the misplaced trust and brought it back to where it belongs, back to the LORD his God.

Bad News

> *"They will have no fear of bad news;*
> *their hearts are steadfast, trusting in the LORD."*
> *~ Psalm 112:7, NIV ~*

Speaking of fear, this verse has been one of the most stabilizing and anchoring verses I ever carried around with me.

I remember the first time I ever read these words. My initial reaction back then was, *"Hey, wow, this is great! No more bad news!"* I figured it meant that now that I had placed my faith in Jesus Christ as my Lord and Saviour, now that I belonged to Almighty God, life would be easy sailing! I was quite thrilled about this revelation!

But before I could continue on with that false thinking for even a second, very gently the Holy Spirit prompted me to look again. It was as if He whispered to my heart, *No, no, that's not what it says. Take a closer look, child.* So, I did. I read it over and over several times, and then I saw it. I saw what was actually written, and when I did, I said to God, *"Oh, I see! I don't have to fear bad news!"* The truth continued to fully sink in and I finally realized exactly what was being said: bad news will still come, but I don't have to be afraid when it does.

As I sat there in my spot pondering such truth, I wasn't so thrilled with what I was reading, but then it began to make sense. Just because I am a Christian, I am not exempt from life's stuff. Just because I had given my heart to Jesus, didn't mean that my days would be all sunshine and roses. The Scriptures don't teach that at all. And it didn't take long for that truth to actually be seen in my own life.

But this verse also showed me the way to put a stop to fear when bad news comes. It showed me the way to thwart the fear that washes over me so quickly. The psalmist says that people like this have a heart that ***is steadfast, trusting in the LORD***. I love the way the King James Version says that ***his heart is fixed***. That's a great word! I think of it as unshakably focused on God! This person knows that nothing can happen to him that is outside of God's knowledge, His will, and His power to see Him through whatever might come his way.

As long as we are in this world, bad news will be a part of life in a multitude of ways. But we don't need to fear it. Every trial is an opportunity to trust. More and more this verse reminds me to keep my eyes and thoughts steadfastly on the LORD, knowing and believing that no matter what, He can and He will take care of me. As the years have gone by, I have experienced this truth more and more. God has shown Himself faithful time and time again.

This precious verse is no longer in my pocket, but it is in my heart and in my mind. It is and always will be, by the grace of God and His enabling, in the way I live. For my good and for His glory.

And as I type, another old pocket verse comes drifting through my thoughts, with which I will close this devotional:

> *"You will keep in perfect peace those whose minds are steadfast, because they trust in you."*
> *~ Isaiah 26:3, NIV ~*

Rivers, Fires and Flames

> *"When you pass through the waters, I will be with you;*
> *and when you pass through the rivers,*
> *they will not sweep over you.*
> *When you walk through the fire,*
> *you will not be burned;*
> *the flames will not set you ablaze."*
> *~ Isaiah 43:2, NIV ~*

When I found this verse again today, I thought of a time some time ago when I was in the car with my kids. They were quite young at the time, as was I – young in my faith, that is. It was one of those moments that in teaching, I was taught.

My four kids and I had been travelling, and we were not too far from home. As we got closer to our hometown, the skies to the west were growing increasingly dark and ominous looking, and my kids were noticing. I told them not to worry, that God was with us, and then I prayed out loud with them, asking God to please keep the storm from coming until we were safely home.

When I finished praying, we drove along in silence for a few minutes, then suddenly one of my boys quietly asked, *"But what if He doesn't, mom? What if God doesn't keep the storm from coming?"*

I can still hear the way his voice sounded, so gentle yet earnest. I can still see his face as my eyes met his in the rear-view mirror. What should I say? What was the answer? As I said, I was still a very new believer; I myself was just learning. So I gave my son an answer, one that at that tender age I more *hoped* was true than *knew* was true. I simply replied: *"Then He will be with us. All the way home, if He chooses to allow the storm to come, He will be with us!"*

This verse, as you see, is spoken by God through His dear prophet, Isaiah. Such powerful promises are packed in here. Promises both good and not so good. Do you see them?

God says **when**. **When** these things happen to you. In a multitude of ways, they will happen and have happened, both to the original audience of this prophecy and to you and I. And everyone in between and all around. It isn't a matter of *if* we come to a place in our lives where we feel like circumstances will surely drown us, but **when**. That's the rather indirect, opposite-of-upbeat promise God makes. The floods and fires will come. But notice this: we must pay attention to the good fact that we **pass through** and **walk through**. This too shall pass! Whatever it is, it won't last forever! It may feel like it, but it won't.

And then there's the even better assurance. ***I will be with you***, God declares. It is the very presence of God that will keep us. The floods and fires and storms of life will come, but they cannot consume us, because God is with us. He will not let them completely overtake us. He will not allow us to be utterly swept away. There are a bazillion verses we could look at to cross-reference that fact. Dozens of Bible narratives, as well as more than a handful of your own stories, I'm sure, to substantiate such truth. By faith and by faithful experience, we believe it. God is with us, even if He chooses to let the storm come before we get home!

I can say that with great confidence now. All those years ago as I drove along with my kids, I was only hoping it was true, especially when the threatening skies became a reality. The last few miles of that trip were pretty rough, but we made it home, safe and sound. And someday, no matter how deep the waters or how hot the fires on this journey we call life, we will make it home. Home to our heavenly abode. Home forever, safe and sound.

My Mighty Warrior

"But the LORD is with me like a mighty warrior."
~ Jeremiah 20:11a, NIV ~

I read these words one morning and hope and strength rose up in my heart! Let's look at them together, okay?

First, I wanna give you several translations of the phrase **mighty warrior**, because they all describe God so powerfully. He is called **a powerful champion** (NASB), **a mighty soldier** (CEV), **most fierce warrior** MSG), **a strong defender** (CEB), and **a mighty, awesome One** (NKJV). Is that great or what?!

Okay, now notice that the verse in almost all Bibles begin with the word **but**. That word just cries out for us to know what comes before. Well, in the previous verses, Jeremiah is at the end of his rope. He is discouraged and beaten down. Literally. His friends are mocking him and plotting against him, his enemies want him dead, and he feels as though even God has betrayed him. In fact, he's even wrestling with the idea of flat-out quitting his whole prophet calling.

That's where the **but** comes in. It's wonderful! Suddenly Jeremiah turns away from his circumstances and sees God! He's like, *Yeah, all that's going on,* **but the LORD is with me**! Can you feel the strength rising up in Jeremiah as he speaks out that truth? Talk about

My Mighty Warrior

encouraging yourself in the Lord! He is with me, so all those enemies of mine will not overcome me (vs. 11b). Because my God is not only *with* me, He is here **like a mighty warrior**! My Defender. My Champion. He will deal with Jeremiah's persecutors how and when he sees fit. Jeremiah can trust God!

I don't know what you are facing this day, but I want to encourage you, don't give up! You may have to wrestle honestly through all kinds of frustrations with the LORD like Jeremiah did. You may feel like quitting, too, but may I say – don't! Please don't quit serving the LORD! Don't quit speaking in His Name! Don't stop sharing and loving and praying for those around you – yes, even those who you feel have betrayed you, those you would consider enemies. Look at the words of Jeremiah. Do what he did. See God! Believe it, He is with you like a mighty warrior! He is with you! You can face whatever the day brings knowing that.

Can I share just one more wee quick thing? Something I love to do is to take these verses and pray them. In the moment you feel defeated, mocked, alone, simply whisper this verse: *"LORD, I know that You are with me! I know that You are my Mighty Warrior! Thank You, Father, for being my Defender! Please show up and help me! Help me now to face this challenge with Your strength and wisdom, in a way that pleases and honors You."* And I assure you, He will.

The Work of a Weaver

*"You shall make a screen for the entrance to the tent,
of blue and purple and scarlet yarns and finely twisted
linen, embroidered with needlework."*
~ Exodus 26:36, ESV ~

This may sound like a rather unusual verse to focus on in the process of my spiritual growth, and if you had that thought, you would be right. It wasn't until I got digging a little deeper, studying the verse in the original language that I saw the beauty and power of these words.

As God gave Moses instructions on building the tabernacle, the place where He would dwell, He was very, very clear on how He wanted it done. It would be beautiful! Every part and piece of the tabernacle would include the most intricate detail. For example, the **screen for the entrance to the tent,** as you see, would be **embroidered with needlework.** Some translations of the Bible, the NASB and the NIV, for example, say it be the **work of a weaver/embroiderer**, respectively. And according to other verses in Exodus, parts of the priest's garments and other pieces of the tabernacle would be made this way (Ex. 27:16 and 28:39, for example). Beautiful shades of colorful yarn, the finest fabrics, finely woven together. Every color significant. Every inch made perfect, according to God's plan and instruction. Woven together by a skilled craftsman.

The word **needlework**, I discovered, is used nine times in the Old Testament (Strong's Lexicon). Eight of those nine times are found here in Exodus, and it means *variegator, worker in colors*. It speaks of weaving together various colored threads, just as the verse says.

But what about that ninth time? Where is it found? Well, are you ready? Because this is a beauty!

In one of David's most "famous" psalms, he says, **"My frame was not hidden from you, when I was made in secret, intricately woven in the depths of the earth** (Ps. 139:15, ESV). See the phrase, **intricately woven**? Well, that is our same word from Exodus, the one used in making the tabernacle! This is the ninth place it is found! How very delightful is that? I love the way the NASB says **skillfully wrought**. And listen to the Amplified Bible: **"My frame was not hidden from You, when I was being formed in secret, [and] intricately and curiously wrought [as if embroidered with various colors]"**. Is that great or what?!

This is amazing to think about. And not just for myself, but for every single person around me and all over the world! Because just as God took great care in designing His tabernacle, so He took the same care designing you and me and all people. Intricate, colorful details went into each one of us. The very hand of God, forming and fashioning us, knitting us together, making us beautiful. We who have trusted Christ as Saviour *are* His tabernacle, individually and collectively, and we have been made as a place for our God to dwell (1 Cor. 3:16;

Eph. 2:22). That is extremely humbling. And extremely joyful! We are indeed ***His workmanship, created in Christ Jesus*** (Eph. 2:10, ESV), and as I consider these things, I can't help but see people a whole lot differently. And I can't help but praise my God, ***for I am fearfully and wonderfully made!*** (Ps. 139:14).

Broken Yokes

> *"I am the LORD your God, who brought you out of Egypt so that you would no longer be slaves to the Egyptians; I broke the bars of your yoke and enabled you to walk with your heads held high."*
> *~ Leviticus 26:13, NIV ~*

I love these words so much. We have all been slaves, held in captivity by sin (John 8:34) and the guilt and shame that it brings. For years I walked through my life with my head down, hoping not to be seen. My own sin, the sin of others and the lies of the enemy held me in that dark place for so, so long. It held me there until the day that Jesus brought me out.

God called the Israelites out of Egypt. He freed them **so that** they **would no longer be slaves** of those cruel Egyptian taskmasters. I love the purpose statement there. There was a reason God did what He did, and that is, **so that**, they would not be slaves anymore! They had been held in captivity for hundreds of years, but now the LORD their God had rescued them. With His mighty arm, with signs and wonders He brought them out (Ex. 13-15).

God **broke the bars of** their **yoke**. The yoke is an apt description for the conditions of their slavery. A yoke, of course, is a wooden and iron bar used on animals to make them move in a certain direction. It kept the animals' heads down, looking toward the fields in which they were plowing, and they could only turn and move as the farmer allowed and directed. With that yoke on them, they were not free in any way.

You can see, then, why the yoke is used metaphorically in scripture to describe subjection, oppression, and slavery such as here in this verse. The Israelites surely were yoked by the Egyptians. The yoke of the power of that enemy weighed the people down. Their cruelty and hatred brought the people of God low in despair and agony.

But God broke the bars of the yokes that held His people captive! He broke the them, and **enabled** them **to walk with** their **heads held high**! That is so great! And please know – this has nothing to do with haughtiness or arrogance, no, this is about dignity and a proper sense of pride in oneself. This is about freedom. In fact, some Bibles actually use those words. Hear this. The New Century Version says *I broke the heavy weights that were on your shoulders and let you walk proudly again!* And the Amplified Bible tells us that God *broke the bars of your yoke and made you walk upright [with heads held high as free men].* Isn't that beautiful? God's people were free, no longer humiliated, controlled, and beaten down.

I love these words so much. I love them because I used to be held in captivity. We all **used to be slaves to sin** (Rom. 6:17, NIV). But Jesus Christ **loves us and has freed us from our sin by his blood** (Rev. 1:5b, NIV). **Through Him** (Jesus) **everyone who believes is set free from every sin** Acts 13:39a, NIV). Jesus brought me out, and you, too, provided you have trusted on Him as your Lord and Saviour, and now we too can walk with our heads held high! All the guilt and shame that condemned us is no longer holding us down like the bars of a yoke. We can live this life with our heads held high, not in arrogance or haughtiness, rather, in joyfulness and gratitude, with the Son shining on us and through us! He brought me out and now I am free and I will walk boldly through this world!

The Airport

*"For you, O LORD, are good and forgiving,
abounding in steadfast love to all who call upon you."*
~ Psalm 86:5, ESV ~

About a week before Christmas one year, I drove to the airport to pick up my son. He was flying in for the holidays and I was *so* excited to see him!

I arrived quite early that day, as I like to do, which meant I had some waiting time. That gave me an opportunity to observe many reunions as one flight after another landed and the folks disembarked from the planes. Some were loud and boisterous reunions, others pretty cool and relaxed. I saw young parents with tiny babies eagerly and tenderly introducing their wee ones to excited grandmas and grandpas. I saw other parents exhaustedly handing over lively toddlers to awaiting family!

It was so cool to watch one gathering after another. Whether they met with laid-back fist bumps or with squeals of delight and smooshy hugs, it was obvious how glad folks were to be connected to one another again. It was the joy of Christmas!

There was one reunion, however, that stood out to me the most. I saw a gentleman wearing a bright blue sweater. He too was waiting for a plane to arrive. He was tall and distinguished-looking; even the way he stood seemed very dignified. He had pure white, perfectly groomed hair and was impeccably dressed. He actually seemed quite unapproachable, cold, intimidating. His face was stoic as he stood patiently and quietly, slightly apart from the rest of the crowd.

But then something happened. People began pouring in. Another plane had landed. The man moved closer, scanning the faces of those arriving. Suddenly a young lady darted out from among those passengers and cried out, *"Daddy!"* Well, that tall, stoic-looking character began smiling so big, it lit up his whole face! He was beaming as he hunched himself down with his hands on his knees, scooching himself short enough to look his girl right in her eyes. Both of them let out a joyful laugh, then in an instant she was completely enveloped in her daddy's arms. All semblance of proper and formal was gone as he welcomed his sweet girl home. He held her for a moment, then they walked away, his arm still around her, laughing and chattering as they made their way down to the baggage area. It was such a moving, tender moment, I almost wished I hadn't seen it.

But see it I did. And I still think of it from time to time because God taught me something in that moment. Something huge. As I watched the scene unfold, I saw a picture of God when I come to Him calling out, *"Daddy! Abba, Papa!"* And the Holy Spirit used such a dramatic contrast in the man's character to show me that sometimes, yes, sometimes I still see God the way I first saw the man in the bright blue sweater. Stand-offish. Uncaring. Distant. Harsh. I didn't even realize that image, that fearful and false image was still in there. It's hard to admit and even harder to share. But share I must.

There are many, many verses that come to mind as I recall this story, but this morning, this very day, as I remember that airport scene, these words of David slipped quietly through my heart. Our God is **good and forgiving, abounding in steadfast love to all who call upon** Him! When I consider all that He has done for me, all He has seen me through, the sheer privilege and pleasure of being in relationship with Him through His Son, Jesus, and to be able to call on Him whenever I want to, it overwhelms my heart!

God is not the way I first saw the man at the airport. No, He is like the second picture of the man. When I run to Him, He is kind and welcoming, and He is, if I may say this out loud, very glad to see me. He calls us to come to Him and He welcomes us when we do. He is gentle with us. He is good and forgiving and merciful and loving. *That* is Who our Father is.

How we view God really, really matters. I mean, Satan, our horrible, lying enemy, will taunt us with wrong thoughts to keep us from running to the Father. He will try to stop us from calling out to Him. Especially when we have messed up. Again. That's why we have to know God truthfully, as He is. So many other things can color our image of our Heavenly Father, so it is important to know Him from what the Scriptures say about Him, not from what we think or what we *think* we know. We cannot assume God is such and such a way based on circumstances or other relationships. We have to get to know Him for Who He truly is, as much as anyone can know

The Airport

Him on this earth. And the only true and accurate way of doing that is reading about Him from His very own Word, talking with Him, listening for Him.

You know what just occurred to me? Thinking back on that young lady at the airport, she had absolutely no hesitancy to run to her father. She called out to him with all of her heart. She squealed with delight when she saw him, and she threw herself wholeheartedly into His arms. Why? Because she knew him! She knew her daddy. She knew that she was loved by him and that he would receive her that way. They obviously had that kind of relationship.

I am so thankful for that moment at the airport. I am extremely grateful for the Holy Spirit and how He is always active in our lives, doing a good work in us, teaching us in the most unexpected ways.

What Do I Do?

"If you don't know what you are doing, pray to the Father.
He loves to help. You'll get His help, and you won't be
condescended to when you ask for it."
~ James 1:5, The Message ~

Many of you may know this verse in other translations. I first learned it in my New International Version, which may have more of a familiar beginning – *If any of you lacks wisdom.*

As I consider this verse tonight it occurred to me: who would this not apply to? Who of us does not experience a lack of wisdom? How many of us could honestly say we never run into situations where we absolutely do not know what to do? I'm pretty sure we're all in that boat together!

But allow me to back up just a schmiddle. What is wisdom, anyway? Well, I found this definition that compares wisdom with knowledge: *"Knowledge is raw information but wisdom knows how to use it. Someone once said that knowledge is the ability to take things apart, but wisdom is the ability to put things together."* And man, do we ever need help putting things back together!

And so, we ask God. Hear that. We ask God. We pray to our Father. We turn to the only One Who can give us true wisdom, who can **guide** us **through a decision or**

circumstance (Amplified Bible), because He knows all things. He knows the way out of every trial and mess we may find ourselves in. When we do not know what to do, He always, always does. We know that, right? We hear it all the time. But does our hearing it and knowing it translate itself into our doing it? Do we ask God for wisdom?

Asking for help isn't always easy. In fact, many times it isn't even on our radar. I mean, asking takes much humility. Asking God for wisdom is in itself an admission that we don't have it. We just don't know what we're gonna do. And that's tough for some folks to admit. More times than not, we like to think we have control and we will figure it out. So, to turn to the Lord, to crave and desire His wisdom? Those are definitely words of humility! It is for sure letting go of our *"I've got this"* attitude.

But you know what I love most about all this? Besides the fact that our Father **loves to help**? And besides the fact that we are totally assured that when we *do* ask for wisdom, ***it <u>will</u> be given to*** us (NIV, emphasis mine). I love the way we are totally assured that whenever we ask, God is *NOT* going to be condescending! That means more to me than I can say.

Our Father, when we come craving His wisdom, is going to give it generously without reprimanding us or making us feel dumb for asking. I love the Common English Bible, the way it says that if we need wisdom, **We should ask God, whose very nature is to give to everyone without a second thought, without keeping score.** Isn't that great?! He is not going to keep track of how many times you've ask about this same problem! He's not going to be all grudgy about it! Why? Because giving is His very nature. It is who He is! He loves us; we are His children. He is not going to criticize us for asking no matter how many times we come. He will welcome us and give us what we so desperately need. I love that! Our God is so, so...other than us!

So that's it. I'll leave you with just two thoughts. One, this very moment, in what way do you not know what to do? What decision? What trial? Have you asked your omniscient Father for wisdom? If not, why not? And two, it would be good to get your own Bible out and read the verses that come before and after this one. Even if you already know them, look again anyway...

But As For Me

*"But as for me, I watch in hope for the LORD,
I wait for God my Savior; my God will hear me."*
~ Micah 7:7, NIV ~

But as for me. I absolutely love the way Micah begins this sentence. No matter what others are doing, in spite of the circumstances of hopelessness and despair all around me, even though there are few that can be trusted and life seems impossible, *as for me, I watch in hope for the LORD.*

Micah has his attention fixed exactly where it needs to be in times of deep and dark distress. He waits for God to move and to act on his behalf and on behalf of all those who belong to Him. He waits for God, calling Him **Savior**. Micah rightly knows and acknowledges that the LORD God is truly is **the God of** his **salvation**. That's the way the English Standard Version says it. **God of my salvation.** I like that. There is no other savior; there is no one who could rescue Micah and the Israelites from the predicament they are in. The same God Who will pour out His righteous judgment will also save. God will not allow the enemy to cause one more ounce of pain that the LORD allows. God will not only mete out His disciple with complete justice, but He will also fulfill every promise of salvation. And so, Micah watches and waits.

As Micah cries out to the LORD, I love the way he calls God his own. **_My God will hear me_**, he says. He is mine! How personal and intimate this is! This dear prophet declares his allegiance to the One True God. His God will hear him. He will answer his cries.

I guess I can simply say that I want to be like Micah. When I first read this verse, I was in some very overwhelming, distressing times. I didn't know a lot of people in my new town, and I certainly didn't know who I could trust. All around me was chaos and uncertainty so the words of Micah pierced through my heart, drawing me in to say the same thing. I had a choice to make, and so I declared, **But as for me**! No matter what other people were doing, who they are reaching out to and depending on, I will wait on the LORD! I will keep watching for Him!

And in my Bible, beside this verse, I wrote down this declaration: *Father, you will hear me! Indeed, You have heard me! You have saved me and Your salvation continues on! I will wait for You, O LORD my God! I will look to You and wait on You all my days!* And then I wrote the verse down on a wee piece of pink paper and put it in my pocket. And I kept it there for many days, moving it from one pocket to another, holding it, reading it, believing it. Making Micah's words my own.

Although there have been seasons where I have slumped with uncertainty, I still keep coming back to this verse. All these years later, I still treasure it. I still hold it close to my heart and it reminds me to live out this truth. And I look back and I see the multitude of ways that my God has saved me. I know he has heard me over and over, time and time again. And when I am tempted to lose hope or to put my hope where it does not belong, or even to look to how other people are making it through, I say to myself, ***but as for me.***

Don't Give Up

*"Let us not become weary in doing good,
for at the proper time we will reap a harvest
if we do not give up."*
~ Galatians 6:9, NIV ~

Oh my, what powerful words these have been for me! I can't tell you how many times I have wanted to give up! Yeah, with a big sigh I tell you that over the years I have gotten tired of doing good. I have found myself discouraged and, well, just over it all. Times when I have whispered to the Lord, *"I quit"*. I'm just being honest with you.

But then the sweet Holy Spirit brings this verse back to mind. It comes with instruction and promise. I am not to become weary. The Living Bible says that I'm not supposed to **get tired of doing what is right.** That's the instruction, and it comes in the context of reaping and sowing.

This makes sense to me. How often have you and I worked so hard on something, serving faithfully, positively, joyfully, and there appears to be no fruit? How often do we do the right thing, make the right choices, only to be slammed down and opposed and nothing seems to change? We have tilled the soil, planted the seeds, weeded and watered in the heat of the day, but still, nothing. That is wearisome! That can cause us to teeter on the precipice of discouragement. But Paul tells the Galatians and you and me – don't get weary!

But why? Why not, Paul? Well, look and see! There is the promise. **We <u>will</u> reap a harvest if we do not give up**! We will! Probably not *when* we want to. Likely not when we think we should. But the harvest will come, whatever that harvest may look like, **at the proper time**. In God's time.

This is a great Greek word. The ancient Greek language had two words for time. The first is *chronos*, meaning time in general. Just regular, chronological time. Minutes and hours and days and such. The second is the word *kairos*, and, according to Vine's Expository Dictionary of the New Testament, it means *a season, a time, a period*. This is a specific, opportune moment in time. It is the right time in time. That's why several Bibles, including the King James Version, transliterates this word **due season**. God assures us that in His perfect time, the harvest will come. That's a promise! But we cannot give up! *I* cannot give up!

And then Paul continues on. He begins the next verse, Galatians 6:10, with **therefore**. Because we can be absolutely assured that good will come from our doing good, and because our doing good matters to God and to His kingdom, and because we do indeed reap what we sow, Paul says: **Therefore, as we have opportunity, let us do good to all people, especially those who belong to the family of believers**, NIV. And wanna hear the coolest thing? That word there, **opportunity**? It, too, is the Greek word, *kairos*. Another issue of God's timing. Perfectly timed spiritual opportunities. And when we do not give up, when take these God-given opportunities, God promises that we most certainly will reap a harvest. We will reap what we sow!

The Soldiers Clothes

"By this everyone will know that you are my disciples, if you love one another."
~ John 13:35, NIV ~

One day I went to one of our local grocery stores. As I got out of my car that day, I saw an elderly gentleman getting out of his. I walked past him and took note of how slowly and carefully he moved. By the time I had run into the store and grabbed and paid for my one thing, the man was at his trunk, pulling out his walker. And this time, I couldn't just walk by.

I stopped to see if he needed help, which he politely declined, and I also stopped because of his clothes. I noticed that this gentleman was wearing pieces of an old army uniform. He had on a coat and a hat with the patches of the military units with which he had served. They showed the places he had been, the wars he had fought, and the training he had received. So not only did I stop to offer my assistance to this elderly man, but also to offer my thanks to a former soldier. I thanked him for his service and told him how much I appreciated all he had done for this country. I shared with him that my husband had been in the army for twenty years, and we talked a few minutes then, sharing with one another that life we had lived.

As I got in my van and set out to drive away, I watched that sweet old serviceman going into the store, kinda bent over and wobbly, using his walker. And I thought, *Lord, he once no doubt stood tall and strong, serving his country with youth and vitality. Yet even here in his old age, he is still a soldier. No matter how much time passes, he will always be a soldier.*

I smiled through tears as I watched him disappear inside the store, and that's when something hit me: I would never have known he was a soldier if not for the insignia he wore. Those patches gave it away. They told a story of who he was and what he had experienced. They drew me in to talk with him awhile.

As I pondered what I has seen, I got to wondering about you and I. I wondered: *what is it about us that tells the world that we, too, are soldiers – soldiers of the cross?* What identifies us with Jesus? What insignia do we wear that shows those around us that we are disciples of Christ?

Jesus tells us here in this verse that people are going to know that we belong to Jesus, that we are His disciples, if we have love for each other. Hmmm…love. Are we wearing that patch well? Is it visible to the world? And in Colossians 3:12, NIV, Paul tells us to **clothe yourselves with compassion, kindness, humility, gentleness and patience.** Peter says something similar, that we **clothe** ourselves **with humility toward one another.** Now *those* are insignia that would surely show we belong to a different kind of army! They are definitely badges of honor, not for you and me, of course, but badges that honor God!

There are so many verses to consider, but let's think on these for now. I hope and pray that people will be able to tell that we are Christians, and that because of the godly attributes we "wear", they will be drawn in to talk with us awhile, just as I was with that old soldier that day. They will be drawn in and we will have the opportunity to share not about *where* we have served, but *Who* we serve. Lord, help us to display Your glory, for all the world to see! Help us to be faithful soldiers of the cross.

Idols

> *"And the idols shall utterly pass away,"*
> *~ Isaiah 2:18, ESV ~*

When I had been saved only a short while, I was in my kitchen one day, talking to God as I was getting lunch ready for my kids. I was basking in the new peace and freedom I had come to know, and I blurted out loud, *"God, there is nothing more important to me than You!"* But as soon as the words were out of my mouth, I had this sudden thought: *am I sure about that?* Could I really declare such a statement? In my spiritual youth and innocence, I knew I meant it when I said it, yet I had this nagging suspicion that made me a little less certain. It wasn't condemnation, rather, it was a loving reality check.

Over the days and weeks that went by, my Father began teaching me that anything or anyone I desire more than Him or place before Him in significance or importance or priority is an idol. And so began a journey with the Lord, a journey of awareness and growth as He lovingly revealed to me the truth of what was in my heart and life. Things that were indeed placed above Him. Gently and clearly, the Holy Spirit brought to my attention things that were definitely idols. And so the journey continues.

One thing I love about this great verse is its absoluteness. God says the idols will pass away, and they *will* pass away! There will be a day when every "god" that we worship on this earth will be gone. They will be completely abolished, destroyed. Everything about them will disappear and be forgotten, and the whole world will know that there is only one God! It is a promise that the Holy One of Israel will fulfill, and for those who do not love and serve Jesus Christ, all who are worshipping idols, which is the context of this verse, it is indeed a very trembly truth!

But when I read these words, something very comforting came over me. When I thought of the work that God and I have done and continue to do to weed out those idols from my life, and to be alert to the possibility of new ones, this reassuring promise brought a sigh to my heart. Because just as this truth is quite threatening, because I am saved, I see it as joyfully promising! And you can, too! The day will come when I stand before Jesus, and all this earthly fuss will be over. All these things that vie for my attention, everything that sneaks in and becomes more important to me than my Saviour, will be cast off! And that is very thrilling to my heart!

'Cause here's the thing: I actually don't want those idols! I truly do *not* want to worship any "god" except <u>the</u> God, my King! But I believe as long as we are here in these bodies in this world, we will be drawn to other things. Less and less, perhaps, but the struggle, the temptation, will be there.

Do you see why this verse is so comforting, then? When God says something, it is as good as done! **And the**

idols shall utterly pass away. And we will stand before our God, worshipping fully, purely, completely, with an undivided heart and with single-minded devotion. All the work will be over. The fleshly struggle will have ended. Nothing will distract us. We will fall at His feet and bask in the glory of the One and Only God and King, our Lord Jesus Christ!

Fire in My Bones

"But if I say,
'I will not mention his word
or speak anymore in his name',
his word is in my heart like a fire,
a fire shut up in my bones.
I am weary of holding it in; indeed, I cannot."
~ Jeremiah 20:9, NIV ~

Poor Jeremiah. He's a mess. He's been through so much. Here in this passage, we find out that he has been beaten and put in stocks because he prophesied according to the word of the Lord and the priests did not like it! (vv. 1-2).

Even though God warned him from the beginning that his calling would not be an easy one, Jeremiah is kind of tired of it. And he sets off on a wee bit of a tirade, even accusing God of deceiving him and overpowering him! (v. 7). He's discouraged by the fact that every time he *does* speak for God, he ends up beaten and ridiculed. (v. 8). It sounds like he's just over it! But only for a moment –

As Jeremiah pours out his heart to the LORD, it isn't long before he turns from the negative, self-pitying, accusatory cries, to the reality of his deepest heart's desire. Even though there are such horrible, negative consequences for being obedient and delivering the prophecies of God, he realized that he just can't stop! He recognizes that if he were to even consider quitting, at the mere thought of not talking about God or speaking in His Name, he could not do it! Why? Because, as this beautiful and powerful verse says, God's word is like a fire in Jeremiah's heart, in his very bones! There's no way he can keep it in! It's not possible for him to hold back from saying exactly what God has called him to say!

Now, needless to say, I am certainly no Jeremiah. Not even close. And to even suggest a resemblance causes me to blush. There are many obvious differences, one of which is the fact that I have never been beaten or thrown in jail or in a pit for speaking in the Name of Jesus. I am no Jeremiah.

However, I must admit that I have had his feelings before. Throughout the years of serving the LORD in writing and teaching and speaking His Word to people, I have gone through some very trying times. Some seasons of my life have been so persistently difficult and the spiritual battles so brutal, that I have, on occasion, thought, *What's the use? Why am I doing this? Is it even worth it?* And then comes that nagging thought that I know comes from the enemy, the adversary, Satan, *I should just quit!*

But then it hits me. I don't want to quit! I can't quit! I love God's Word so much, and there is nothing in this world that I want to do more than to teach it and write about it and talk about it! I can't not do it! I realize that is terrible grammar, but it's true! And this is also where I feel like Jeremiah. This is where his words become my words. No matter the cost, no matter the risk or the troubles or the trials that may come, I will speak! If I even consider not mentioning God anymore, **His word is in my heart like a fire, a fire shut up in my bones. I am weary of holding it in; indeed, I cannot**!

Jeremiah had a very specific message during a very specific time. It was a message of repentance. He spoke to the wicked, wandering people of Israel, those who were supposed to be following God with all their hearts but were not. They were following hard after other gods, caught up in their wickedness, worshipping every kind of idol. So God, in His rich mercy, send Jeremiah to call the people to return to the LORD, warning them of the coming judgement if they remained in their sin. Not a popular message for certain, yet it was truth and it had to be told.

Truth be told, I must tell you that God has called all of us to speak for Him and about Him. Jesus told us to **go into all the world and preach the Good News to everyone, everywhere** (Mark 16:15, TLB). He has called us to share that Jesus is **the way and the truth and the life**, and that **no one comes to the Father except through** him (John 14:6, NIV). That is not always a popular message in this day and age, but it must be told! Regardless of the resistance we get. Or how much persecution or ridicule. The hope of the love and mercy of Jesus Christ and the coming judgement must be told to all people. I pray that His Word would be burning within us, and that we will boldly proclaim it at all cost!

Grace in the Wait

"Oh LORD, be gracious to us; we wait for you.
Be our arm every morning,
our salvation in times of trouble."
~ Isaiah 33:2, ESV ~

With the enemy tearing through Israel, and their sights now set on Judah, specifically Jerusalem, the people of God cry out to the LORD to show them His mercy. **Be gracious to us**, they plead. They long for deliverance from this brutal and ruthless enemy. And they plead not only for their deliverance, but for the annihilation of the enemy.

And so, they **wait**. Strong's Concordance says this word has a feeling of expectancy. They expect God to show up. It's about faith. They keep waiting and watching. Not just gonna give it one quick glance and one short prayer to see if God will do something and then give up hope. No, they wait with anticipation. They believe that He can and He will. They are lingering, watching, and hopeful of what God will do. I like the way the NIV says **we long for you.** Their whole hearts and minds are set achingly on the LORD.

And speaking of that longing and waiting, we sure can't miss what they are actually saying: **we wait for <u>you</u>.** These folks who have been so rebellious, who have turned to idols for help, who have beckoned other nations to support and intervene, who have completely relied on their own ways, *finally* turned to and are calling for the only one who actually has the power to save! To really save! That is, the LORD their God! And they need Him to be gracious to them.

So, they ask God to **be** their **arm every morning** and their **salvation in times of trouble.** The arm of God, mentioned this way, speaks of His power and authority and might. In fact, the Amplified Bible adds this after speaking of the arm of God: **that is, their strength and their defense.** I love that! God's arm has the power to move mountains, to destroy and to conquer and to truly save! The enemy here is likely the Assyrians, and up to this point, they seem to win every battle. They thrive on their evil and seem to be unbeatable, as God temporarily permitted. And in this frightening and chaotic upheaval, the Israelites need God!

And one more thing. As is always the case, when I see someone crying out to the LORD to be gracious to them, and to show Himself strong on their behalf, the obvious other-side-of-the-coin is that they are recognizing that they are not able to save or defend themselves! They do not have what it takes to fight this battle and rid themselves of such a formidable threat.

You might be going through a battle right now, too. It could be that the enemy is on the horizon, ready to attack, which he so often is. You may even be able to look around and see the destruction that he has already caused. That's when we have to cling to these words. Make them your own, **O LORD, be gracious to** me; I am waiting *for you. Be* my *arm every morning,* my *salvation in times of trouble.*

He Will Provide

*"Then the LORD said to Moses,
'See, I have chosen Bezalel son of Uri,
the son of Hur, of the tribe of Judah,
and I have filled him with the Spirit of God,
with wisdom, with understanding,
with knowledge and with all kinds of skills –
Moreover, I have appointed Oholiab son of Ahisamak,
of the tribe of Dan, to help him.
Also I have given ability to all the skilled workers to
make everything I have commanded you.'"*
~ Exodus 31:1-3, 6, NIV ~

There is a lesson that God began teaching me very early on in my walk with Him. I saw it all throughout the scriptures, and definitely experienced it first hand in my own life. The lesson is this: what God requires, He supplies.

Some years ago, I began leading women's Bible studies. After a short while, I knew that the Lord was calling me to begin writing my own studies, which, in the beginning, I fearfully and reluctantly did. But over time I grew to love doing it. It was and still is such a joyful part of my life. I realized that those years spent reading my Bible every day had purpose. I didn't know it then, but as time went by, I saw what God had been up to. He had been equipping me to write those verse-by-verse studies. He had supplied in me what was required to be obedient to that call. And that is obviously the most important part of it. But there was more piece to the story, something very practical.

During that time I had a very old computer that I used to write my lessons, and it was beginning to give me problems. It was becoming quite a frustration, because it often stalled my completion of the weekly studies, and my husband and I just weren't in a position to purchase a new one. Not right then.

One day there was an unexpected knock on my door, and when I answered it, there was a sweet friend of mine. She stood there on my porch with a big smile on her face, wanting to talk to me. She shared a wee story about how she and her husband had received some unexpected money, and the next thing I knew she was putting an envelope in my hand, a bank envelope filled with cash! Enough money, she explained, to buy a new laptop.

I was shocked, and at first I tried to refuse this extremely generous gift. I was not one to ask for help, or to ask for things from people, so when this gift came it was a complete surprise, and I wasn't sure what to do. But my friend insisted, telling me that God had put me on her heart when the money came. She said that she and her husband, who have both insisted on their anonymity, realized it wasn't theirs at all, rather, they were to give it to me. So, with much gratitude, with tears and hugs, I accepted her abundantly kind gift.

When my friend left, as I was thanking and praising God for His remarkable goodness toward me, these verses came back to mind. My kids and I had just read them the night before, as well as the whole passage and chapters around them. As we read, I had shared this lesson that God was beginning to teach me because it is such a perfect example –

The verses I am writing about are, as you see, from Exodus chapter thirty-one. The chapters before this are God-given instructions for building His tabernacle and all the furnishings, as well as the priestly garments and instructions for the priest's consecration (Ex. 25-30). It was a lot of work that needed to be done. Very specific, elaborate work, and it had to be done *exactly* as God commanded.

Now, I don't know if Moses ever thought about this, but did he wonder, as God showed him how these things were to be made, who would do the work? Did that ever cross his mind? Did he wonder how it would all get done? Whether he did or not doesn't matter, of course, because God knew exactly what He would do. God wanted the work done, and, as always, He supplied everything the people needed to do it. He supplied not only, well, the actual supplies, but also the hearts and hands that would do the work. Beginning with the anointing of these two guys, two of my favorite guys, Bezalel and Oholiab.

God Himself raised these men up and filled them with the knowledge to do what He commanded. And not just the two of them, no, God also, as you see, gave **ability to all the skilled workers to make everything** He **commanded.** But most importantly, aside from all the wisdom and skill, God gave them His very own Spirit! Chosen by God, Bezalel, Oholiab and the whole spirit-filled team, in the power of the Holy Spirit, would get done all that God had commanded them to do!

Do you see how good God is? He didn't just give the orders then leave them on their own to figure it out. Of course He didn't! Our God is so good and so gracious, and His plans are so perfect! He provided what He required.

Now, I realize that I am no Bezalel or Oholiab. But I am, in my own wee way, helping to build God's temple. He has filled me with His Spirit and enabled me to do what He has called me to do. He has given me all I need. Including a laptop.

You know what? I couldn't wait for my kids to get home from school that day so long ago. I had to tell them what God had done for me! When they arrived, we all went out back to our swing, and as they ate their snack, I told them delightful stories about worn our computers and a surprise visit, about an envelope filled with money, and the excitement of a shiny new laptop that would enable me to get the work done that God had given me to do. I joyfully explained as best I could about how the Spirit works and moves among His people, and the importance of obedience to His promptings. And I reminded them about Bezalel and Oholiab, and how God always, always gives us everything we need to serve Him in the way he commands. What God requires, He supplies, I told my babies that day, and over the years I've seen it happen time and time again, both in His Word and in my own life. What God requires; He supplies.

The Promise Goes On

"As long as earth endures, seedtime and harvest,
cold and heat, summer and winter,
day and night will never cease."
~ Genesis 8:22 ~

Very early one morning I got up and went out for a walk. I headed west down our main street, and when I got near the edge of town, I turned around to head back toward home, and when I did, I was quite literally stopped in my tracks.

As I said, it was very early, so it was still quite dark when I left home. As I walked west, that's what I saw. The dark sky. But when I turned around, it was the perfect moment when dawn is just slightly beginning. The sky had begun to brighten and a few stray clouds were turning the most glorious, glowing colors as the sun, still hidden from my little corner of the world, reflected on them. They stretched out across the sky as though they were joyfully introducing the brilliant sun that was about to rise!

It was such a dramatic difference from what I had been looking at that I had to break my stride and stand there a moment. I needed to look back to the west and see how dark the sky still was, then look again toward the east. I'm glad the streets were quite empty so I could thoroughly take in this moment. I mean, it's not like I've never seen the early parts of a sunrise before, but this time it became for me a powerful reminder of this promise that God made so, so long ago.

When Noah and his family came off the Ark after the flood waters had receded, God told Noah that He would never again destroy every living thing as He had just done. And then God made this promise. This covenant. While the earth remains, these normal patterns of creation and life would go on. We see them all the time, don't we? Spring comes, and the seeds are planted. Autumn, and the crops are brought in. The seasons pass, transitioning from one to the other like clockwork. Day turns to night, night into day; the cycle goes on and on.

But how many times do we just not notice? I mean, sure, our alarm clocks go off and a new day begins. But think about it. Every time the sun rises and sets, when we get out of bed and lay our heads down at night, we are witnessing and experiencing first-hand the faithfulness of our God! Each time we put our winter coats away because the air has warmed up or get them back out because the temperatures are falling, when we see the trees dressed in fresh, new blossoms or beautiful leaves of yellow and red, with every sunrise and sunset, cold wind and snowflake, blistering heat and summer rain, we can be sure that God is keeping His promise! These things have never stopped, since the moment He spoke these words to Noah to this very day.

The morning that I stood on the sidewalk watching the treasure of a new day dawning, it made me smile. Not only because of the beauty, but also because I thought,

The Promise Goes On

yep, God is keeping His word! He is faithful! He is doing what He said He would do, and oh my, He is doing it well!

This verse and this unexpected lesson on the streets of my town had such an effective impact on me. I pray it does for you, too. As we move through our rather ordinary days, we need to remember how truly faithful our Father is. He is trustworthy and dependable. Every word He has spoken comes to pass. Not a single promise will go unfulfilled. Our God will do what He said He will do! Always, we can count on Him. Always. Let's be mindful of this truth that is played out all around us every day. Watch for it. Take notice. Let it encourage us, so we can then encourage others.

Torn Hearts

"Rend you heart and not your garments."
~ Joel 2:13a, NIV ~

I have a confession to make. I never really understood this verse, because when I first read it, I didn't know what the word **rend** meant. But imagine my delight when I discovered it simply means *to tear*! (Dictionary.com). It was delightful because that's when this verse started making sense.

Joel is a prophet who, in the midst of a national crisis, is calling God's people to repentance. And please notice I said *God's people*: those who were once walking with Him. Those who were supposed to be faithfully following and serving Him. They had drifted deep into idolatry, so through His prophet, Joel, God calls the Israelites to **return to me with all your heart, with fasting and weeping and mourning** (Joel 2:12). All visible evidence of a repentant heart. And then Joel goes on to say, speaking for God Himself, **rend your heart and not your garments.**

See, in those days, tearing your clothes was a sign of deep grief and mourning. People tore their clothes because they were overcome with sorrow, including sorrow over sin. But God knew very well, that folks could quite easily tear their clothes and not be affected at all in their heart. They could surely go through the outward motion of repentance, but just not mean it. And so, God says, in effect, *forget about tearing your clothes, it's your heart that must be torn! Yes, tear your heart!* This means to be completely, genuinely broken over sin. It is grief from the inside out. Not just a going-through-the-motions display of insincere "repentance". Not because it's what's expected or part of the culture of the day. You have to mean it! **Return to** the LORD **with all your heart**! Let your heart be broken over sin and come back to God.

The morning I found this verse, I was praying about it when suddenly something occurred to me: you can't tear hard things! Think about that. If you have a heart that is hardened and calloused it cannot be torn. You cannot rend **a heart of stone**, as Ezekiel calls it. I guess what I am saying is that you have to care that you are sinning against God. You have to desire to return to Him and make things right. It has to matter! But here's the greatest thing: even that is a work of God, and He can help you with it. God says through His guy Ezekiel, **I will remove from you your heart of stone and give you a heart of flesh** (Ezek. 11:19, 36:26). He will give you a heart that is soft and tender and teachable, sensitive to the Holy Spirit.

I really have to show you the rest of my pocket verse now, the whole thing, because it is so powerful and hope-filled –

"Rend you heart and not your garments.
Return to the LORD your God,
for He is gracious and compassionate, slow to anger
and abounding in love,
and he relents from sending calamity.
~ Joel 2:13, NIV ~

Do you love that? God's mercy and compassion are promised to you! I assure you, if you allow your heart to be torn over your sin, if you return with a broken and contrite spirit, you will be met with mercy so great, with love and grace unlike anything you've ever experienced. He will forgive. God loves you so much, too much to leave you there in your sin. Please, dear one, forget about what it looks like on the outside. Please, rend your heart and return to the LORD your God!

Seeing

*"So from now on we regard no one
from a worldly point of view."*
~ 2 Corinthians 5:16a, NIV ~

I was having a conversation with my Bible study ladies one day about sharing the love of Jesus with folks around us, as well as potential obstacles that keep us from sharing. As we talked, this old pocket verse popped into my mind, and when it did, I also remembered what I had learned from it: we actually have to *see* people and to see them rightly.

Now, this may seem crazy obvious, because we most likely come across dozens of people every day. They are all around us, everywhere we go. But do we really *see* them? And if so, *how* are we seeing them? Paul tells us quite clearly in this verse that we are to **regard no one from a worldly point of view.** The Message Bible says that **we don't evaluate people by what they have or how they look**, and the J. B. Phillips New Testament says that **our knowledge of men can no longer be based on their outward lives**!

Wow, right?! The obvious other-side-of-the-coin is, that if we don't see people from a worldly or fleshly perspective, we have to see them from *Jesus'* point of view! If we start seeing those around us through the eyes of

Christ, I am certain that our compassion and love for the lost and the weary will explode. I just know it will help us to show and to share the love of Jesus wherever we go.

And please notice the part of the verse that says ***from now on***. This phrase caused me to ask myself, *From when on?* Well, the verse right before this one says ***and he died for all, that those who live should no longer live for themselves but for him who died and rose again***. We who love Jesus are those who live. We are alive in Christ, saved by grace through faith and should no longer be living for ourselves but for Him Who saved us. And when we are living for Jesus, then we need to be about His business, bringing others to Him. And in order to do that, we have to *see them!*

As I type this wee devotional, I suddenly recall an experience that Jesus had. Mark records this for us, that ***when Jesus landed and saw a large crowd, he had compassion on them, because they were like sheep without a shepherd. So he began teaching them many things*** (Mark 6:34, NIV). Jesus saw those people. He saw them with a heart of compassion. He saw them as they were: lost and in need of a shepherd. And so He taught them. Although we are not given the specifics of that particular teaching, we can safely assume that with much love, Jesus told them that He is the good Shepherd that they were in need of and they were to follow Him. He would have shared the good news! (That's what I'm guessing, based on the Gospels.)

On the day that I talked with my girls we agreed that we must pay attention! We must notice those around us! In the stores, in the check-out line, in meetings, at work,

Seeing

at the gas station, in your neighborhood, and yes, even in your own home! Smile. Make eye contact. Let someone go first. Take time to ask a question then really listen to the answer. Say something nice; give someone a compliment. Ask God to give you a sincere, caring heart. 'Cause this isn't a put-on act of flattery. This is genuine kindness that comes from a heart that loves Jesus and wants the world to know that Jesus loves them, too!

I'm gonna be honest, this isn't always going to be easy. It certainly doesn't come naturally. No, this is a beautiful work of the Holy Spirit in us, so let's pray that He will grow this kind of seeing in us more and more. Father, we pray that you would indeed help us to see people, to really see them as You do. Not based on their outward appearance, but to see them through Your eyes. Help us to see with Your love and compassion. Help us to see them as those who need a relationship with You. Amen.

Believe

"Let not your hearts be troubled.
Believe in God; believe also in me.
~ John 14:1, ESV ~

This is another one of those most "popular" verses, yet I never tire of hearing these sweet words of Jesus. Although I may not know you, nor do I know what you might be facing this very day, I do know enough about this old world to know that you may be facing *something*. Some troubling thing. And although I am in and of myself quite helpless in helping others as much as is needed, the joyful and most beneficial thing is that I can bring you to Jesus, to His most powerful and effective Word! And so I bring you to these words – **do not let your hearts be troubled**.

Jesus spoke these words to His dear disciples just hours before He hung on the cross. He knew very well that their lives would be thrown into great chaotic confusion. He knew that their world as they knew it would be shattered, that what was once "normal", would never be the same again. He knew they would be filled with fear and sorrow and complete bewilderment. Jesus knew.

They had, in fact, already experienced many troubling things. Jesus had just revealed that one of their very own was actually a traitor, and that very soon they would all deny Him and leave Him. And the most shocking: that He was going to leave them. My heart aches just typing those words! Of course, they would be troubled!

But what amazes me, what causes my heart to rejoice with love for Jesus, is that there, on the eve of His very own death, He was bringing comfort to others! He was giving them assurance and strength as He said, **Believe in God; believe also in me**. No matter what you see, guys, no matter how ugly things get and how hopeless they appear, believe! Trust Me, just as you trust God the Father! Have faith in both of us! **Believe**, and **do not let your hearts be troubled**!

It would be good to know what this word **troubled** means. According to Strong's Concordance, this Greek word, *tarassō*, means *to cause inward commotion, to take away calmness of the mind; to strike one's spirit with fear and dread; to render anxious and distressed*. All of these feelings were surely headed toward the disciples, because they couldn't see the bigger picture. They couldn't yet comprehend the fullness of God's plans and purposes for what was about to happen, so Jesus exhorts them to trust!

As I mentioned at the beginning of this writing, I do not know what you are going through right now. I don't know if you are experiencing something that has completely destroyed your "normal", but Jesus knows. And further, I don't know what may be causing that inward commotion and distress, but I do know where to take you to ease some of your fear and anxiety – right back to this familiar and loving verse. Jesus knew before time began what you and I would be facing today, and so He spoke these words and had them written down so that they would last forever, so they would reach the ears and the hearts of His disciples so long ago, but also to your very own ears and heart today. And like the disciples who sat with Jesus that night, we can't always see the greater plans and purposes for what God allows in our lives, and we may not be able to understand, even if we were told, but the message still rings out from the pages of scripture, a message that I pray will settle deep into our hearts this day: ***Believe in God; believe also in me.*** Trust Him, precious one; He's got you!

He's Been So Good

*"Return to your rest, my soul,
for the LORD has been good to you."*
~ *Psalm 116:7, NIV* ~

This is one of the easiest, sweetest verses I have ever carried around with me.

I know I've talked often of struggles and hardships in life, and perhaps you wonder why. Well, it's not because I'm a negative or pessimistic person, not at all. The reality is, life is hard. We are never promised an easy road. Now, if you're one who has had a relatively calm and peaceful life, free from much trauma and trouble, then I am most delighted to hear that! I am truly happy for you! But for others – for *most* I dare say, myself included – life has not been easy. And someday, as the Lord allows and enables, I might just share my story with you.

For today, though, I will sum it up like this: if not for the love and care of my Saviour, I would not be here. I know that. He has been with me all along. All through my life my God was there. He has been part of my story since my story began. I know that, too. Now, I didn't always know it. I didn't always believe it. But I do now. With all my heart. I believe and I must praise Him for His faithfulness and for His patient, persistent love!

You may wonder what in the world does all that have to do with this verse. Well, it does, in fact, have everything to do with it. It is a reminder, a forever, absolute reminder from God Himself to my very soul, that he has been good to me! Through it all, He *has* been good to me!

As I recall the story of my life, I see my Father there, watching over me, providing for me, caring for me in countless ways. Oh, don't get me wrong, there have been days that are so dark I've come very close to forgetting that. Even doubting. Days where my faith has wavered and waned and I've gotten angry and bitter and filled with self-pity. But, by the grace of God and the sweet presence and prompting of the Holy Spirit, my focus shifts once again, and He helps me to see and recount all the good in the midst of the difficult. In fact, He enables me to see how the difficult *becomes* the good. Sometimes, it really does.

And I have learned over the years that it is good and helpful to preach these things to myself in order to gain the truth and the perspective that I need. Because the truth is, God *has* been good to me! He *is* good to me. No matter how tough life is, I see Him at work in me and in my circumstances. Sometimes it's only by faith that I see it, but that okay, too. When my soul is in angst and despair, when I am frazzled and frenzied, I recall these words of David, and I am calmed. I have peace when I tell myself, "**Return to your rest, my soul, for the LORD has been good to you!**"

First the Songs

> *"After consulting the people,*
> *Jehoshaphat appointed men to sing to the LORD*
> *and to praise him for the splendor of his holiness*
> *as they went out at the head of the army, saying:*
> *'Give thanks to the LORD,*
> *for his love endures forever.'"*
> *~ 2 Chronicles 20:21, NIV ~*

I've gotta confess, when I first read this verse, it totally made no sense to me. I just didn't get it. Being very new in my faith, and quite unfamiliar with the concept of spiritual battles, Jehoshaphat's plan did *not* make sense to me! But let me begin at the beginning…

King Jehoshaphat was king of Judah, and in this moment, he was surrounded by a **vast army** of enemy soldiers (2 Chron. 20:1-2, NIV). They were closing in fast, and when the king was told about it, yes, he was scared, yet he did the best thing he or anyone could do. **Then Jehoshaphat was afraid and set his face to seek the LORD, and proclaimed a fast throughout all Judah. And Judah assembled to seek help from the LORD; from all the cities of Judah they came to seek the LORD** (2 Chron. 20:3-4, ESV). There could be no wiser move to make than to turn to the LORD when the enemy surrounds you and you are afraid!

After much prayer and fasting, some encouraging words from an old prophet of God and a time of worship, the battle was nearing. The prophet, Jahaziel, told the king and all his people not to **be afraid or discouraged of this vast army. The battle is not yours, but God's** (2 Chron. 20:5-19, NIV, which I *really* encourage you to read!). He gave them their marching orders with promises of God's protection, and the next morning, acting in total faith in the words God had given through Jahaziel, they set out.

That morning, as they went out to face the enemy as directed by the LORD, King Jehoshaphat encouraged the people to have faith in the LORD and in His prophets and promised them that they will be upheld and successful. They will need to cling to that trust in God when they saw how vast the enemy armies were! And then, after talking things over with the people, as we read, **Jehoshaphat appointed men to sing to the LORD and to praise him for the splendor of his holiness.** * That is awesome and beautiful!

But what got me the day I first read this was the *position* of the singers: they went out at the *head of the army!* Yikes, right?! This is the part that didn't make sense to me. Why in the world would you put the singers first? Why not your strongest, most valiant soldiers with the best weapons available? It made me glad I do not have a great singing voice! :)

But as I read and re-read this passage, as I pondered and prayed, it began to make sense. Maybe not logistically from a military point of view, but spiritually speaking, it totally began to make sense. Because

First the Songs

it suddenly hit me: the praise *does* come first! Praise *is* our greatest weapon! And in this account, so great was their faith in the word of God, so strong their belief in Him, that He would do what He promised to do, that they praised Him for the victory before the battle even began! They took God at His word. When the enemy had them surrounded and completely outnumbered, God has already won the battle. They only had to step out in faith and praise His glorious Name, giving Him thanks for His enduring love.

This is actually the same for you and me. The more time I spend walking with God, the more I understand this. Every day I get up out of bed, I walk out onto a battleground. We have an enemy, the devil, who is very real and very ruthless. But we have a God Who is all-powerful and all-loving, Who walks with us and lives in us and **greater is He who is in you than he who is in the world** (1 John 4:4b, NASB). And I know that in Christ, the victory is already mine, because Jesus has already won! He has already defeated Satan, and the final reality of that defeat is absolutely certain. And that is something to praise Him for! To know that He is with us. To know and believe that He fights for us. So yeah, the praise does come first!

No matter how big the battle is, when I lift my voice to worship Him, things begin to change. I'm not pretending the enemy isn't there, no, I am doing what Jehoshaphat did: I am setting my face to seek the LORD. And when I do that, it redirects my eyes, my thoughts, my heart away from the fear of the battle and toward the One Who has already overcome. When I praise, the battle and the enemy become smaller and smaller in the glory of God's majestic presence. I can walk into every day, knowing that victory is mine.

    I'm gonna be honest: this is another one of those lessons that I needed to learn and learn and relearn. But the more I practice it, the easier it becomes. Again, I must say, this is not an avoidance tactic. It is not us burying our heads in the sand or covering up our pain or pretending the battle isn't real. Absolutely not! Because sometimes, yes, sometimes, the praise is no more than a whisper. A desperate, wondering, tear-filled whisper. Yet even that God hears and responds to. Even that re-directs our hearts toward the Healer and Helper of our souls and situations. It reminds us of the goodness of God. And you know what? This reminds me of another very similar lesson from another favorite pocket verse, which just happens to come from this very same narrative...

The NIV uses the phrase **for the splendor of his holiness. Other Bibles, the NASB, for example, translate this rather difficult Hebrew phrase as **those who praised him in holy attire.** I just wanted to make note of this and encourage you to dig in a little on your own, reading various translations and paraphrases, as well as Bible commentaries.*

Powerless

> *"Our God, will you not judge them? For we have no
> power to face this vast army that is attacking us.
> We do not know what to do, but our eyes are on you."*
> *~ 2 Chronicles 20:12, NIV ~*

As you can see, this verse comes from the same battle scene that we just left. Since I already shared the context, and I trust you have read through it for yourself, I will simply share the lesson that God taught me through this particular verse, part of the prayer of King Jehoshaphat.

First, the king talks with the LORD about the Moabites and the Ammonites who are coming up against him, crying out to God to judge them. And then he says one of the greatest and most important things a person could say. He acknowledges that he, that they as a nation, **have no power**. They were indeed powerless to face such a vast army, and Jehoshaphat knew it. But do you see how awesome that is? The first step in any battle, I have learned, is knowing that we, that *I*, do not have the strength to fight it alone. But oh, my, how often I try! And how often I fail! So what an awesome example Jehoshaphat is for me! What a humble, godly man he is, to admit that he needs God to deal with his enemy because he is unable, on his own, to do so.

My powerlessness comes at different levels. Sometimes the situations are such that I literally am not physically strong enough to deal with it. As the Israelites were that day, I feel surrounded. The enemy is indeed stronger and larger than I am. He is coming at me from every side and I am not able to face him alone.

Other times, quite often, actually, it is more of an emotional powerlessness. It comes from too much for too long. Weariness. Exhaustion. *Not another thing! Please, God, not one more thing. I have no fight left.*

But if you find yourself in that place, it's okay. You're gonna be okay. This is where God wants us to be. No fight left. No independent, self-sufficient fight left. In and of myself, I can do nothing. Time to do what Jehoshaphat did: acknowledge this to my Almighty God. I turn to Him and say, *Lord, you must deal with my enemy, because I have no power.* And you know what? He hears me. And He gives me the strength I need. He gives me power. *His* strength. *His* power. *His* strategies and ideas and wisdom. He leads me through. And sometimes He simply fights for me. Sometimes, suddenly, the battle is just over. All glory to my God and Saviour!

And then there's the last part of the verse. This next sentence is embedded in my mind and in my heart. Seriously, I can't tell you how often I pray, *"God, I **don't know what to do"**,* without the rest of the verse coming to mind, ***"but** my **eyes are on you."*** Man, that is so comforting! My eyes are on You, God. Not on myself. Not on my dilemma. Not on the enemy. No, upon You! Stop and think what a big deal that is! My focus is on all-knowing, all-seeing, all-wise God!

However, as comforting as that is, these words have also been sweetly convicting. Because sometimes when they roll through my mind and off my tongue I am stopped. As I hear myself speak this verse to the Lord, I have to ask myself, *"Are they? Are my eyes really upon You? Right now, in this moment?"* And truthfully, sometimes the answer is no, no they are not. But do you see then, how gracious the words become? As I read them or recall them, Jehoshaphat reminds me where my focus needs to be and I am helped. I turn my eyes toward Jesus and I know that somehow, someway, someday, everything is going to be okay.

Where, When and Why

*"For God so loved the world,
that He gave His only begotten Son,
that whoever believes in Him shall not perish,
but have eternal life."*
~ John 3:16, NASB 1995~

This is, as you may know, not only the most well-known verse in all the Bible, but also one of the most beautiful, filled with love and grace and promise. Who can understand a love like this? Who can ever fully comprehend such sacrifice? There is so much to write about; so much to rejoice over that God sent His only Son to die for us so that we who believe will never be lost, but will have everlasting life! We will live with Jesus forever!

One day as I pondered the glory of this verse, a different thought came to mind, one that may seem rather trivial in light of the weight of this truth that lay before me. You see, my mind kept wandering to the time and place in which Jesus first spoke these words. What exactly is the context? Where was He and with whom was He speaking? And why, why did Jesus share this amazing truth? Well, the answers are really quite wonderful! Let me show you with this verse:

"Now there was a Pharisee, a man named Nicodemus who was a member of the Jewish ruling council. He came to Jesus at night and said, 'Rabbi, we know you are a teacher who has come from God...'"
~ John 3:1-2a, NIV ~

Isn't that wonderful? Nicodemus was a Pharisee; a ruler of the Jewish people. He was wealthy, educated, and very religious. The Pharisees were strict keepers of the Law, legalism at its best. They were all about rules and rituals, all outward works. And most importantly, they came from the "right" family. They were descendants of Abraham. It was this Jewish heritage and their rule-following that led the Pharisees, including Nicodemus, to assume that they were assured a place in heaven. This was their basis for believing that they had a right relationship with God.

But then came Jesus. Nicodemus had been watching Him. He had seen the miracles and heard His teachings. He had seen how the people were responding to this Man. There was just something about Jesus. There must have been a strange stirring in Nicodemus's heart, way deep down, a curiosity, something that drew Him out one dark night.

Why he came at night is only a matter of speculation. There are different theories, the most common being that the dark of night was the perfect cover. This was, after all, a great risk that Nicodemus was taking. Being seen with Jesus would not have been a good thing.

But you wanna know something? We could spend ages pondering the "whys", when all that ultimately matters is that he came to Jesus. In spite of his position and education and genealogy, he came. In spite of the risks, he came. He came with questions and curiosity, bewilderment even, and Jesus received him.

Can you just picture it? This is only my imagination, but can you picture the dark and quiet night? Can you see the dim flicker of the oil lamp and hear the hushed tones of the two men as Jesus proceeds to tell this Pharisee the *real* way to eternal life? Is this thrilling your heart yet? I mean, how many times have you read or heard John 3:16? How much sweeter it is when you put this scene together!

I can't help but wonder what Nicodemus felt in that moment as Jesus said, **For God <u>so</u> <u>loved</u> the world!** The whole world, Nicodemus! Not just an elite few, no, the whole world! So much so that **He gave His only begotten Son that whoever believes in Him, shall not perish, but have eternal life**! Whoever <u>**believes**</u>, Nic! Not whoever keeps the Law. Not only whoever descends from Abraham. Whoever believes as Abraham did, *they* will have **eternal life**!

Oh, what was that like there where they sat? It may have been real dark outside, but, man, the light of the truth was glowing all over the place as Jesus gently and patiently taught. Perhaps even in the heart of that curious and confused Pharisee. And the light of that truth is still glowing in our lives today. Oh, how I thank Jesus for taking the time to talk with this sweet man!

But why does any of this matter, you may ask. Who cares when or why or to whom Jesus first said these words, as long as He said them? Well, because keeping scripture in context is always important, and in this case, I especially love it because it shows one of the tenderest, most loving moments with Jesus. Just look at it. Although the Pharisees were totally against Jesus, Nicodemus went anyway, and Jesus took time to have this quiet, intimate conversation with "one of them". He may have been very tired Himself, yet He was there, gently leading this seriously misinformed leader out of the darkness and into the Light. Jesus didn't shout these words from a mountain top. He didn't first make sure a large enough crowd was listening or choose the "right kind of person" to share it with. Jesus just isn't like that. No, He spoke these words to one who came to Him. One who came seeking and searching for answers to his questions in the middle of the night. Jesus shared this most beautiful, life-giving truth to one who didn't allow his religion or education or pride to keep him away. I love that!

For God so loved the world, Nicodemus. Including you! I wonder if – in all the legalism and rules and "making it look good" on the outside of the world of the Pharisees - anyone had ever told Nicodemus that before. I wonder if it had ever occurred to him or made its way into his heart. The God you claim to know, Nicodemus, the God you are so desperately trying to serve, in your own strength and power and way, HE LOVES YOU! So much so, that I am here for you, says Jesus!

I want you to know this, too. It's always good to check our own hearts. No amount of religion will save you.

And who's your daddy just doesn't count. It's personal, just you and Jesus. It is only through Jesus Christ that true salvation comes. God sent Him to die in your place because He loves you that much. And just as Jesus was willing to sit with Nicodemus and answer his questions, so He is willing to sit with you and answer yours. So go to Him, dear one, and ask your questions! Go to His Word and let Him speak life-giving truth to you today.

Old Clothes

> *"I delight greatly in the LORD; my soul rejoices in my God. For he has clothed me with garments of salvation and arrayed me in a robe of righteousness."*
> *~ Isaiah 61:10a, NIV ~*

Now, before you turn the page because you think there has been an editing error, let me assure you, there is not! Yes, I have written about this verse already, but I learned something more from these words as time went by, and it is on my heart to share it with you. So, with that said...

One day, as I was studying this verse again, the Holy Spirit brought to mind something kind of sad. A bad habit that I had. A wrong way of thinking. Sometimes, instead of "enjoying" my new clothes of salvation and righteousness, I would find myself once again wrapped up in garments of guilt and robes of regret. Rather than having my eyes focused on Jesus, on what He has done for me and who I am in Christ, they were drawn back to the past, where all those old memories live of who I used to be. I would easily be overcome with all that mess and begin to wonder how God could forgive me and how "someone like me" could ever serve Him. Does that ever happen to you?

Well, if it does, if you keep thinking about your past in a negative, critical way, the things you've done and the person you were, I assure you, it is not God bringing it up! Because, although He is omniscient and forgets nothing, *He chooses to forget!* But don't take my word for it. It's always best to let God speak for Himself. Listen to what He says through His prophet Isaiah: ***I, even I, am he who blots out your transgressions, for my own sake, and remembers your sins no more*** (Isa. 43:25, NIV). And God speaks similar words through Jeremiah and the writer of Hebrews, saying, ***for I will forgive their wickedness and remember their sins no more*** (Heb. 8:12, from Jer. 31:34b, NIV) Furthermore, He clearly states that ***as far as the east is from the west, so far does he remove our transgressions from us*** (Ps. 103:12, NIV). Micah tells how God ***will tread our sins underfoot and hurl all our iniquities into the depths of the sea*** (Mic. 7:19, NIV). And I could never forget to mention the awesome words from Paul: ***Therefore, if anyone is in Christ, he is a new creation; the old has passed away; behold, the new has come*** (2 Cor. 5:17, ESV). And just one more, if I may, so we absolutely know, ***there is now no condemnation for those who are in Christ Jesus*** (Rom. 8:1, NIV). No condemnation!

However, our enemy, Satan, does bring the up the past. He does attempt to condemn us. In Revelation 12:10, we see Satan called ***the accuser of the brothers and sisters***. And that's what he does. He accuses us. He would love for us to stay back there in the "who we used to be". He is glad to hand us that tattered old coat of guilt and shame and regret, and even help us put it on! But please hear me, precious child of God, those garments of guilt and robes of regret do not fit you anymore! They don't fit me, either! That's not who we are! We have new clothes to wear! We are children of God, and when we are all wrapped up in matters that have long ago been settled by the forgiving, cleansing blood of Jesus, we become quite ineffective in our service for Him. It's hard to live and to work in the present when we are all tangled up in the past! So let's keep our eyes fixed on Jesus Christ and what He has done for us and in us. Nope, you're not perfect, but you are forgiven, and our good Father is at work in you making you more and more like Jesus!

Something I am learning to do when the enemy comes at me with this, "yeah but remember when" nonsense, is to turn it back to praise. I don't even respond to that old accuser, rather, I pull that garment of salvation and robe of righteousness tightly around me, I run to my Father and shout, *"Thank You, Lord, for rescuing me from that! Thank You that by Your grace I am not that person anymore! I praise You for forgiving me and calling me Yours. I delight greatly in You and rejoice because You have saved me. I worship You because I have been declared innocent, made right with You through the finished work of my Saviour, Jesus Christ! Amen and Amen!*

However...

Why We Remember

*"I remember the days of old;
I meditate on all that you have done;
I ponder the works of your hands."
~ Psalm 143:5, ESV ~*

So, hmmmm. There are many other verses coming to mind after that last writing. Verses such as this one. Because while it is true that we must not ponder our past in negative, self-deprecating ways, the scriptures clearly tell us that remembering where we've come from and considering God's good works is actually a very powerful and important thing to do. It is beneficial to our spiritual health! As in this old pocket verse, for example, where David is clearly stating that he is remembering days gone by. He is thinking a lot about what God has done for him in the past.

And there are so many other verses that talk about not only remembering your past, but why it is valuable to do so! I'd like to share just a few with you.

In Deuteronomy 6:12, NIV, it says, **be careful that you do not forget the LORD, who brought you out Egypt, out of the land of slavery.** This command/warning that God gave the Israelites most assuredly applies to you and me today. We cannot forget God. We can't forget that we were once enslaved to sin and it was God alone

Who brought us out. It's good and proper to remember where we came from so we never lose sight of God's saving grace in our lives, especially when He blesses us so abundantly. That's what was going on in the context of this verse. Moses was describing the excellent land the Israelites were headed into, the abundant provisions and blessings that God would be pouring out upon them, and once they got there and were enjoying those blessings, they mustn't forget Him! He alone is their one true God. It was He Who brought them out and would lead them into such goodness. This remembering keeps us humble. And grateful. And dependent on the Lord, with praise ever on our hearts and lips!

And then Paul, when dealing with the issues of the church on the Island of Crete, said this: **Remind the people...to be obedient, to be ready for every good work, to speak evil of no one, to avoid quarrelling, to be gentle, and to show perfect courtesy toward all people** (Titus 3:1-2, ESV). Obviously, this is the way all believers *should* live, but I love that Paul gives a specific reason for the command. Hear what he says next: **At one time we too were foolish, disobedient, led astray, slaves to various passions and pleasures, passing our days in malice and envy, hated by others and hating one another** (Titus 3:3, ESV).

Yikes, eh?! That is who we were before we were saved! All of us. So, Paul is basically telling them to remember who they were. They needed a reminder to treat unsaved people well, because they once behaved *exactly* the same! Don't forget that. This remembering keeps us from being judgmental and hateful to those who do not yet believe, or to believers who are at a different level of maturity. It keeps us from showing favoritism and prejudice toward *anyone*. Because, as Paul also reminds them in verse four and five of Titus 3, (and I absolutely *love* these verses), yes, they used to behave that way, **but when the kindness and love of God our Savior appeared, he saved us, not because of righteous things we had done, but because of his mercy.** Wow, that is so good! It's good to remember where you came from, who you used to be, and that it was *only* the mercy of God that saved you from that way of life! So be nice to people! Have mercy on others, as the Lord has had mercy on you.

And just one more. A wee bit of a different angle. As I was typing, I thought of Revelation 2:4-5, ESV, where Jesus says: **"But I have this against you: you have abandoned the love you had at first. Remember therefore from where you have fallen; repent and do the works you did at first."**

This is part of the letter to the church in Ephesus. They had forsaken their first love, which, of course, is Jesus. The Amplified Bible puts it like this: **you have lost the depth of love that you first had for Me.** The passionate fire that once burned so hot and bright for the Lord was now only a barely-glowing ember. And that loss of love would negatively influence everything else in their lives. Their service, for example, where once was ignited with love for Jesus, was now more like a dutiful obligation. So they have to remember where they were before they fell! They must look back and figure out where they had begun slipping, back to the place where they had taken a wrong turn; a turn away from their first love. A thorough, honest self-analysis for reasons of the potential need of repentance is *always* a good thing! Always!

That is my wee list for today. We do not look back at who we were before we knew Jesus as Lord and Saviour in order to chastise and condemn ourselves or to feel sorry for ourselves. We do, however, think back from time to time to remember the glorious works God has done for us, how He kept us, called us, saved us and blessed us with uncountable blessings! We remember because it brings praise and glory and honor to the One Who so richly deserves it!

We ponder our past in order to recall that it is only the mercy of God, that He sent His Son Jesus to die in our place, that we are who we are now. It gives God all the "credit", and us the right perspective on other people. It reminds us to show the same mercy and kindness to them that God has shown to us!

And lastly, we remember as a warning. Like a caution sign. Don't go back there again. Don't act like who you used to be! We look back to see where we are now and check for any drift in direction or half-heartedness of passion or motive. Return, repent, ask the Spirit to re-ignite that flame and then get back to work! Run to and stay with your first love, and that is your Savior, Jesus Christ.

The Centurion Heard

"...the centurion heard about Jesus..."
~ Luke 7:3a ~

There's a lot to talk about in this account of the centurion's servant. All sorts of good thing to consider. But sometimes the very best parts are the simplest. That's what I found here, in this small portion of a verse.

So, this centurion, the Roman officer, had a servant, a bond slave, who was highly valued by him (Luke 7:2). This guy was very important to the centurion; in fact, the New King James Version actually says that he **was dear to him.** And this poor servant, so valued by his master, was sick to the point of death. Imagine how the centurion would have felt watching so helplessly as his servant grew more and more ill. But then he heard about Jesus.

There it is. He heard and he sent for Jesus, asking Him to **heal his** dear **servant**. Now, I know you know what the word **heal** means, but I love to look at the definitions in the original language. There is something sweet about it. So, this Greek word, *diasōzō*, according to the Vine's Expository Dictionary of the New Testament, means *to bring safely through a danger; to make completely whole.* And Strong's Concordance says something similar: *to bring safely through; to save thoroughly.* I love those definitions! That is what the centurion was asking Jesus for.

Now, if I may jump ahead to the end of the story, I'll tell you that Jesus did heal the servant. It's quite a wonderful story, and I encourage you to take some time to read the whole thing. You will see that Jesus did bring the man safely through this dreaded illness. The servant was made whole again. He lived. And all because the centurion heard about Jesus.

As I said, there are so many things to talk about in this passage, but when I read it one morning, this is the part that my heart was drawn to. It just seemed so simple. First we have death and despair. Then we have hope and life. And right in the middle is Jesus. The centurion heard about Jesus, and everything changed.

How he heard, I don't know. I guess it doesn't really matter. What's important is that somewhere, sometime, somebody told him. Somehow, word got out. That's what matters. It matters that this Roman officer knew he was helpless to deal with such a crisis, and it matters that when faced with a moment like this, he thought of Jesus. It matters that the Name of Jesus, the Name that is above every name, was talked about. Because that is how hope, healing and life came. Because of Jesus.

> *"Consequently, faith comes from hearing the message, and the message is heard through the word about Christ."*
> *~ Romans 10:17, NIV ~*

He Has a Home

> *"While Jesus was in Bethany in the home of Simon the Leper, a woman came to him with an alabaster jar of very expensive perfume, which she poured on his head as he was reclining at the table."*
> *~ Matthew 26:6-7 ~*

This is such a beautiful story, the account of the woman who poured perfume on Jesus' head. But one morning, when I heard these words, something else caught my attention, something that comes before the real story, and it really made me smile. I couldn't get past the part about Jesus being in the home of Simon the Leper!

Isn't it great how the Bible records that fact so simply and matter-of-fact? It's just kinda stuck in there. No real attention is drawn to it; no big deal is made of it. It's just what Jesus did. It is simply a geographical location that sets the stage for the real story.

But to me it is so much more than that. I think it *is* a big deal, and I feel this way because it is a beautiful picture of who Jesus is. Seriously, when I read that sentence, not only did it make me smile, but it also caused me to think: *Well of course He is! Where else would He be?!* Sure, He could have been down at the country club, hob-nobbin' with the highfalutin people. He could have been hanging out with the Pharisees and the Teachers of the Law. But no, Jesus was here in the home of Simon the Leper.

Not much is known about this guy. Scholars speculate that it is quite likely that Jesus healed this man at some point. And that makes total sense. Somewhere, in some moment in time, as Jesus was walking along, He heard a man crying out, *"Unclean, unclean!"*, as was the requirement, according to the Levitical Law (Lev. 14:35). But it makes me wonder, when Simon saw Jesus come near, instead of crying out, *unclean*, did he instead cry out, *"Jesus, Jesus!"* Or did Jesus just step into this man's life and touch him and make him clean? Perhaps someday, I will ask him! :)

There is another very cool thing that struck me about this situation. I realized that now Simon has a home! Before Jesus came, he would have always been on the outskirts of town, always separated and alone. Leviticus 14:46, ESV, says: ***He** (the leper) **shall remain unclean as long as he has the disease. He is unclean. He shall live alone. His dwelling shall be outside the camp.*** Imagine how lonely and isolated that would have felt. So detached from the world. Unable to be with family and friends. Unable to go to the temple to worship God. Unclean. Alone. Outside the camp.

Those are some incredibly heart-wrenching words. So sad. But it's alright, no need to be upset, because it's all different now! Simon has been healed and he is allowed to be among the people! And, according to this verse, now he has a home. And Jesus is here with him, reclining at his table. It's truly no surprise, but it sure is beautiful! This is just my own thinking, but I picture Jesus and Simon laughing and talking and eating together, enjoying a good meal. Close friendship and a joyful time with one another and with all the folks who were there that day. Who Simon used to be is a distant memory. Now he is clean. And Jesus came to his home to spend some time with him.

You know, I've been thinking about this, my mind drifting here and there, considering what this all means to me and what I can learn. As I try to imagine this moment before the real story, it makes me love Jesus even more. See, it causes me to remember the years before Jesus walked into *my* life, if I may word it that way. It makes me think about how He healed me and how His touch changed my life forever. I am clean. I am whole. And I think how even now, as I sit here in my favorite spot at my dining room table, I know He is here. With me. That never ceases to amaze me. Jesus was willing to come for me and to me and now He dwells in me (Gal. 2:20, Eph. 3:17). Such a sinner am I. So unclean was I when He found me. Such struggles I still wrestle with. Yet here He is. But where else would He be, right?

And may I say one more thing? My minds also strolls forward to an unknown moment in time, a day when there will be another table that Jesus and me and Simon the Leper will be gathered around. You'll be there, too, if you are a follower of Jesus. Folks from all the ages, all those who the Master touched and made clean, all who were once sin-sick and isolated and separated from Him, but now have been forgiven, cleansed and brought near in a close, personal relationship with Him, will be there.

There comes a day when we will be with Jesus, and we have this encouraging invitation from Revelation 19:9 that will on that day be fulfilled: **Blessed are those who invited to the marriage supper of the Lamb**! What a glorious, indescribable time that will be!

Meanwhile, as we wait, Jesus remains our example. Just as He spent time among the sick and the weak, among the "unclean", He calls us to do the same. We are to invite others to this banquet so they, too, can recline at the table. Jesus taught in Luke 14:13 that we are to **invite the poor, the crippled, the lame, the blind.** And the only way we can invite them is to be among them, just like Jesus was. Simon the Leper and Jesus were reclining at the same table that day because in a single moment in time they met one another. There are so many others out there waiting to meet Him, waiting to be spiritually healed, longing for a true home with Him...

The Servants Knew

> *"When the master of the feast tasted the water now become wine, and did not know where it came from (though the servants who had drawn the water knew), the master of the feast called to the bridegroom..."*
> ~ John 2:9, ESV ~

As I read this passage of scripture, the account of the very first miracle of Jesus, something actually struck me funny. Within this extremely important event, filled with rich and deeply profound significance, I noticed the servants.

What made me chuckle is that parenthetical statement, **though the servant who had drawn the water knew.** The "important" people did not know where this really good wine had come from. Not the master of the feast. Not the bride nor the bridegroom, nor the most highfalutin guest in the crowd. Of course, Mary knew. And Jesus' disciples at some point figured it out. But it was the servants who got to actually participate in the miracle first-hand!

I got to thinking about these guys. I tried to imagine how this all played out. I got to wondering about all the details of a servant's life, details that positioned them to be a part of such a miracle. Yeah, I know it was their job, but perhaps if we look a little closer, we might see more than that.

As I dug into the narrative, I first noticed in verse five that Mary **said to the servants, 'Do whatever He tells you.'** (These are, by the way, the last words we will hear Mary, the Mama of Jesus, speak. Let that sink in a moment. Mull it over in your mind until it settles deep into your heart and all the way out through your hands and feet! It's pretty huge, eh?!)

Anyway, as I was saying, **Mary <u>said</u> to the servants.** She *said*. It is the Greek word *lego*. The regular word for speaking. Not shouting. Not yelling across the room. Not grumbling about good help being hard to find. She simply spoke to them, which tells me that they were standing nearby. They were close. Physically available. They positioned themselves in such a way that they would be able to hear the needs of the guests.

They also had to be present. Have you ever been somewhere physically, yet totally missed what's going on around you? Your body is in one place, but your heart and mind are somewhere else? It happens to all of us, I believe. But it seems these guys were there, fully present, alert, watching, listening. They were engaged. Mary said, "**Do whatever he tells you**." I can almost see them immediately turning their eyes to Jesus, waiting to be given instructions.

The servants also had to be willing to serve. Again, I acknowledge that yes, that seems like an obvious point because it is their job, but there is evidence of a willingness to do their job well. They didn't just have a servant's position; no, it appears that they also had a servant's *heart*.

As they looked to Jesus for direction, He told them **"Fill the jars with water."** (v. 7). And they obeyed Jesus' command. They obeyed immediately, and they obeyed well. Not only did they fill those water jars, but **they filled them to the brim**! (still v. 7). They weren't slack in their work. They didn't hit the three-quarter mark on those big old jars and suddenly have a "that's good enough" attitude. No, they went all the way, filling the jars to the point where they couldn't hold another drop! That took some work!

But I wish I could have seen their faces as they began the work. Did they look at one another with confusion? They were obedient, yes, but as they poured the water, were they also somewhat perplexed? Did they whisper among one another, "*I don't know either, but let's see what happens!*" Was there a thrill of anticipation fluttering around in their tummies? I mean, they were real guys, so it could be.

And I further wonder, did a wee bit of dread wash over them as they heard Jesus say, **"Now draw some out and take it to the master of the feast."** (v. 8). Yikes, eh?! They had put *water* in those jugs! "*And You want us to give it to our boss?*" But again, they obeyed. They dipped a ladle into that water, and as they poured it into a smaller pitcher something happened. If there had been any trepidation in them, surely it now turned to an awestruck disbelief! It was wine! It wasn't water anymore, it was wine! And as Jesus had commanded, they **took it to him**. They gave it to the master of the feast. And **when** *the master of the feast tasted the water now become wine, and did not know where it came from (<u>though the servants knew</u>), the master of the feast called the bridegroom and said to him, 'Everyone serves the good wine first, and when people have drunk freely, then the poor wine. But you have kept the good wine until now.'* (vv. 9 and 10).

Wow, right? Again, my eyes turn to those servants. What must they have been thinking and feeling? No doubt they remained calm and quiet and professional, but man, they must have been busting on the inside! Did they glance over at one another again, only this time with faces shining with amazement? Did they whisper to one another, *"What just happened?!"*

I'm sure the master, once he tasted the wine and gave his approval, would have then ordered those guys to go ahead and serve it to all the guests. And they would have. And as they poured each cup full of wine, their hearts would surely have been overflowing with joy and wonder.

Yep, it was just another day on the job. Another wedding to tend to. Yet this ordinary day, and this ordinary event, turned out to be, no doubt, the grandest day in the servant's lives. They were chosen to participate in a glorious miracle of Jesus! They were standing by, available, present, ready to listen and willing to serve. Even if it didn't make sense. Even if the job was a big one. And they knew, when no one else did, where the wine had come from. I don't know how they couldn't have kept from going and worshipping at Jesus' feet.

Throughout all of this pondering, I've been thinking about you and I. I'm wondering, as servants of Jesus, what might we get to see? Could it be that throughout our ordinary days, doing our ordinary jobs, Jesus will use us too, to participate in His wondrous works? Could it be that as we serve together the way the guys in this account did, we will experience acts of God that cause us to say with delight, *"What just happened?!"* I believe we will, especially if we heed those words of Jesus' mama – "**Do whatever He tells you...**"

What Shall I Do With Jesus?

"Pilate said to them,
'Then what shall I do with Jesus who is called Christ?'"
~ Matthew 27:22, ESV ~

Throughout the scriptures, there are some extremely thought-provoking questions, and this particular question is actually the most important one you will ever have to answer.

At the time of the Passover, it had been decided by the chief priests and the elders of the people to put Jesus to death, so they handed Him over to Pilate, the governor (Matt. 27:1-2). **Now at the feast the governor was accustomed to release for the crowd any one prisoner whom they wanted** (Matt. 27:15, ESV), and so, when a crowd gathered before him, he presented Barabbas to them. And he gave them a choice. Barabbas? Or Jesus? Which one would be set free? Which one would be executed by crucifixion? And according to the Gospel of Mark, **the chief priests stirred up the crowd to have him release Barabbas instead** (Mark 15:11, ESV). And so, the crowd chose Barabbas to be set free.

Pilate was caught up in the midst of this frenzied uproar. But his wife had warned him not to **have anything to do with that innocent man** (Matt. 27:19). Pilate himself knew the Jews' motives and reasons were not right in wanting Jesus dead. But there he stood with this angry mob railing on him, insisting that he release Barabbas, a known criminal. And so, he shouts back to them the most important question ever spoken: ***"Then what shall I do with Jesus...?"***

It was just a question. It was something that needed to be asked as Pilate tried to rid himself of the responsibility of Jesus' death. But I wonder if he had any idea of how crucial a question he had actually posed to the crowds that day. What will you do with Jesus, Pilate? Well, we know what he did. **He had Jesus flogged, and handed him over to be crucified** (Matt. 27:26, NIV). Pilate released Barabbas, but turned Jesus over to be killed. And they **crucified the Lord of Glory** (2 Cor. 2:8).

The morning that I read this, as I continued on with the rest of the account of Christ's death, burial and resurrection, this question continued to linger in my mind. It still does. In fact, this question reverberates through all of time, into the lives of every single person who has ever lived, is living, and will live. There is not a single soul who will not have to answer it.

Many who are reading this have already dealt positively with this question. You have answered it by declaring with your mouth, ***"Jesus is Lord"***, believing ***in your heart that God raised him from the dead***, and you are saved! (Rom. 10:9-10, NIV). What have you done with Jesus? You've acknowledged that He is Lord of lords and King of kings! And He is your Saviour! The matter is firmly settled.

But sadly, way too many have answered this question another way. Just as Pilate listened to the crowds that day, many today listen to the shouts of this world and of our own selfishness. We, too, are so caught up in chaos, pulled so many directions of false teachings and lies and we have a decision to make! What will you do with Jesus?

The world has rejected Him. They try to explain Him away and they call Him a liar. They have denied Jesus, criticized Him, minimized Him, and mocked Him. However, no matter what people do in an attempt to destroy the truth of Who Jesus is, one thing they cannot do is ignore Him. They cannot stop the fact that one day we will all see Him face-to-face (Rev. 1:7, ESV). There will most certainly come a day when **at the name of Jesus every knee will bow in heaven and on earth and under the earth, and every tongue confess that Jesus Christ is Lord, to the glory of God the Father** (Phil. 2:9-11, ESV). No one can stop the eternal truth that Jesus is alive, and that He is the only way of salvation (Acts 4:12). No amount of distortion or covering up of the Gospel can hinder it from going forth. How we answer Pilate's question is quite literally the difference between life and death. Because here's the thing: there really is a heaven and there really is a hell, and praise God, there really is a Way! And his Name is Jesus!

So, in this very moment, based on Pilate's ancient yet lingering question, I will ask you: what will you do with Jesus, who *is* Christ?

Come!

"The Spirit and the bride say, "Come!"
And let the one who hears say, "Come!"
Let the one who is thirsty come;
and let the one who wishes take the
free gift of the water of life."
~ Revelation 22:17, NIV ~

I cannot describe how thrilled I was one morning as I read these words. I mean, I'd read them so many times before, but I just hadn't seen it. But this day, the sweet Holy Spirit opened my eyes and I saw!

See, there are only four verses after this, then God's written Word is completed. And here, this close to the end of the Book, in one of the very final thoughts that God wanted written, is a final plea of salvation! John wrote down one more time an invitation to come.

As I have studied this verse, it seems there are some differing opinions about the first sentence. While most, if not all scholars I read agree that the rest of the verse is a definite invitation to unbelievers to come to Jesus, to accept His free gift of salvation, they think differently about the first part. Some say it is a cry for Jesus Himself to come back. I can totally see that. Others believe that these words are also referring to unbelieving people to come to Jesus and be saved. While both responses are good and acceptable, whichever way it is, we know for certain that this is a cry of the Spirit for people to be saved. And that is why it was so joyfully surprising to me that morning so long ago.

The Apostle John had been banished to the island of Patmos for his unceasing preaching of the gospel. While he was there, God gave him visions of the future end of days. He was given visions of many strange and troubling events. He saw catastrophic situations as God's wrath was poured out and His judgments were executed. John saw the final battle between God and Satan, and was shown the agony and horror of men as they refused to repent. He heard and saw things that we can't even begin to imagine, even though we can read his very words. God instructed John to watch and write down this prophetic revelation.

On the other side of all that, this dear apostle was also privy to the most hallowed of places, being witness to visions more wonderful than our hearts could bear to see. He was given visions of Jesus Himself! And John even tells us that, **"When I saw Him, I fell at his feet as though dead"** (Rev. 1:17, NIV). He **looked, and there before** him **was a door standing open in heaven** (Rev. 4:1)! Guys, he saw **a throne in heaven with someone sitting on it**! (Rev. 4:2). Which was, of course, God Himself!

And the wonders continued. Oh, the sights that he saw and the sound that he heard! Music resounding through the corridors of heaven! Angels gathered around the throne, singing, praising our God! Voices of countless numbers singing in angelic harmony. Prayers of the saints calling out to the Lord and trumpets and harps and worshipping creatures. He tells of the glory and majesty and holiness of Jesus, the One worthy of honor and glory and praise!

Yes, John was given this whole revelation, both the joyful and the dreadful parts. And after it was all done, after he witnessed death forever defeated and Jesus Christ reigning as King of kings and Lord of lords, The Holy Spirit breathed these words into John's heart: tell them to **come**! Can you even imagine such grace? Do you get how absolutely awesome this is? It is amazing and delightful! All these things will surely take place. All the wrath. All the judgments. It *will* come to pass. But not yet. There is still time. So John pleads from the fifth to the last verse – not only in the book of Revelation, but in the entire Bible – **whoever is thirsty, let him come**! While you still have the opportunity, come and **take the free gift of the water of life**. God in His compassionate love and grace, gives one last call to be saved!

And dear one, I must join this plea today...please come to Jesus! Come and receive the free gift of salvation that Jesus offers. He is the only One who can offer such a gift and it is available to you now. I pray you feel the thirst for this Living Water, a thirst that cannot be quenched apart from a relationship with Jesus Christ. I pray you will acknowledge that deep longing within you and that you will come. The invitation is still available.

Do you see how thrilling this verse is, then? Our God, from the beginning of His Word to the end, is all about bringing us back to Himself. It is always about reconciliation, and the Spirit says, "**Come**"!

Precious reader, if you have never accepted this free gift of salvation, why not answer this call now? Simply acknowledge that you are a sinner in need of a Saviour. Ask God to forgive your sins. Tell Him that you believe by faith that His Son, Jesus Christ, died on the cross for your sins, that he was buried, and that He rose again. Then praise Him, dear one, because you have been forgiven! You are now a child of God!

And for you who just asked Jesus into your heart and life, and for all readers, it would be good for you to take some time to look up these verses in your Bible or on your Bible app. They are very important verses regarding salvation. Read them, study them, find someone to ask questions about them, and pray. Ask the Spirit to teach you, and He will...

Isaiah 55:1-2
John 4:13-14, 7:37-39
John 5:24
Acts 4:12, 16:30-31
Romans 10:9-10
2 Corinthians 5:21

One Last Thing...

One final thought...

This was to be the end of these pocket verses, but as I was closing, something came to mind that I must write down. Earlier in this wee book I talked with you about Genesis 8:22, NIV, how God continues on with the covenant promise He made to Noah: *"As long as the earth endures, seedtime and harvest, cold and heat, summer and winter, day and night, will never cease."*

In that devotional I focused on the promise. There is, however, another truth within that beautiful verse, and it is this truth that I must tend to before I close.

Please notice that in this verse it is written: **As long as the earth endures.** That's the NIV, as you see. Other Bibles say things like this: **While the earth remains** (NASB), **So long as the earth exists** (CJB), and **during all the days of earth** (YLT).

This phrase clearly indicates that there is a time frame involved. All of these seasons and cycles will indeed go on as God has ordered, as they are right now, but only as long as earth endures. There will come a time when it all comes to an end.

In the verse right before this one, God says that He will ***never again kill off everything living as I've just done*** (Gen. 8:21b, The Message). Well, how did God just kill everything off? With the flood. God drowned the entire world, except, of course, for Noah and his family. But now He promises that He will never, ever again destroy everything that way.

But what God does *not* promise is that He will never again destroy the earth at all. He does not promise that it will last forever. **As long as the earth endures**, God says. There will indeed come a day when this old earth will be destroyed, in fact, Jesus Himself talked about it. In Luke 21:33, NIV, He said, **heaven and earth will pass away**. (You should definitely check out the rest of that verse!) But this time, when it does pass away, it will not be with a flood.

The Apostle Peter actually compares the past destruction of the earth with what is to come. By the inspiration of the Holy Spirit, he writes:

> *"They deliberately forget that long ago by God's word the heavens came into being and the earth was formed out of water and by water. By these waters also the world of that time was deluged and destroyed. And by the same word, the present heavens and earth are reserved for fire, being kept for the day of judgment and destruction of the ungodly. The elements will be destroyed by fire, and the earth and everything done in it will be laid bare."*
> (2 Peter 3:5-7, 10b, NIV)

I know those are not easy words to read. They are not easy to fully fathom. But they are, in fact, true. This earth is not a forever thing, and it will, someday, be destroyed once again, this time by fire. A time will come when time will end. But for a believer in Jesus Christ, this actually offers much hope, because we are promised so much more than what we see here and now! See, Peter further goes on to say, in verse thirteen of this same chapter: ***But in keeping with his promise, we are looking forward to a new heaven and a new earth, where righteousness dwells.***

Yes, God promised these things long before Peter spoke of them. Hundreds of years earlier, through His prophet, Isaiah, God said: ***"See, I will create new heavens and a new earth. The former things will not be remembered, nor will they come to mind*** (Isaiah 65:17, NIV), and that when He makes this new heaven and new earth, He declares that they ***shall endure before*** Him (Isaiah 66:22, NIV). These will for certain last forever! And God further promises that in that day, not only will the heavens and earth remain, but also that His ***salvation will last forever, and My righteousness will never fail*** (Isaiah 51:6b, NIV). Those are the promises to which Peter refers.

And meantime, as we await that glorious day, there is still hope in the here and now. Because between the flood and the fire, there is grace. This is the day of grace, with full opportunity to believe on the Lord Jesus Christ and be saved. You, too, can share in this eternal home with our Righteous Ruler.

As always, I would encourage you to read the passages I wrote about here. Read all of 2 Peter 3. In that chapter, look and see…when will the heavens and earth be set on fire and dissolved? What kind of people ought we to be in the meantime and why is it important? Give it some thought. Ponder it as you also consider that every promise God has ever made will surely come to pass.

Father, we thank You for Your enduring Word. What a hope and a blessing to know that every word You have spoken will be fulfilled. Please, Father, give us the courage, the fortitude, the wisdom to believe what You have written, to understand it, to live it, and to share it boldly and kindly with those You place in our lives. Help us to stand strong and true on this unshakeable foundation! In the precious and powerful Name of Jesus, Amen!

Conclusion

Well, dear friends, that is all for now. We have come to the end of this wee book of pocket verses. There are so, so many more that I could have included, and, God willing, I will write about them, too, someday. For now, though, I pray these that are written will have brought you some encouragement, some hope and some help. Maybe some instruction, too. I pray that you will be hungry to feast on the Word of God for yourself, and that when you do, you will find great delight in what you read. The Bible truly ***is living and active and full of power!*** (Heb. 4:12, Amplified Bible). I encourage you to take some time each day to sit with your Bible, a notepad and a pencil, expecting the Lord to speak to you. He will meet you there and you will find the greatest treasures. Your heart and mind will be transformed as you fill it with truth. It will be a transformation that will, no doubt, begin to affect the way you live and love and serve. People will notice, and you, too, will have a story to tell.

Now if I may, I would like to close with one final verse, a prayer for you and I as we continue on in our spiritual journey...

> *"Open my eyes, that I may behold*
> *Wonderful things from Your law."*
> *~ Psalm 119: 18, NASB ~*

Until next time,
With love and for His glory,
Sherry

www.ingramcontent.com/pod-product-compliance
Lightning Source LLC
Chambersburg PA
CBHW031720260226
40320CB00039B/667